Boom Basics

Dutch Financial Supervision Act

Mr. R.A. Stegeman

BOOM BASICS IS EDITED BY

Prof. mr. T. Hartlief
Prof. mr. A.W. Heringa
Prof. mr. C.J.H. Jansen

eleven
international publishing

Published, sold and distributed by Eleven International Publishing
P.O. Box 85576
2508 CG The Hague
The Netherlands
Tel.: +31 70 33 070 33
Fax: +31 70 33 070 30
email: sales@elevenpub.nl / www.elevenpub.com

Sold and distributed in USA and Canada
Independent Publishers Group
814 N. Franklin Street
Chicago, IL 60610, USA
Order Placement: +1 800 888 4741
Fax: +1 312 337 5985
orders@ipgbook.com / www.ipgbook.com

Eleven International Publishing is an imprint of Boom uitgevers Den Haag.

ISBN 978-94-6236-140-9
ISBN 978-90-5454-838-6 (e-book)

Printed in The Netherlands

Table of Contents

I Introduction

In our daily lives, we are all active on the financial markets. We have a mortgage, a payment account, various insurances, a pension and possibly investments in shares on the stock exchange. The financial crisis of 2007 has shown the importance of the functioning of the financial markets for our economy. The crisis eroded public confidence in the financial sector. This explains the increased public's and government's attention to the supervision of the financial sector.

Usually, the government's attention results in regulation, which is translated into legislation and supervision. For the financial sector, this relates in particular to the Financial Supervision Act (**FSA**).

This act is relatively unknown and therefore unloved by most lawyers and law students. In my opinion, this is completely unjustified. Dutch law cannot be more extensive, complex, dynamic and therefore more challenging than the FSA. The purpose of this Boom Basics Dutch FSA is to make the FSA more accessible to interested parties.

I would like to thank my colleagues Aron Berket, Auryn Bokma and Koen van Leeuwen who also contributed to this edition. This Boom Basics Dutch FSA describes the state of affairs up to 1 January 2020.

1 Position in Dutch law

Financial supervision law

The Financial Supervision Act (FSA) is one of several sources of 'financial supervision law', by which we mean 'the law for the supervision of the financial markets and their actors'. Other sources are *e.g.*:

- Pension Act;
- Sanctions Act 1977;
- Foreign Financial Relations Act;
- Securities Giro Act;
- Consumer Protection (Enforcement) Act;
- Savings Certificates Act;
- Money Laundering and Terrorist Financing (Prevention) Act;
- Audit Firms (Supervision) Act;
- Financial Reporting (Supervision) Act; and
- Trust Offices (Supervision) Act.

Overlap with other fields of law

In addition, the FSA overlaps with other fields of law such as administrative, criminal and civil law:

- Many of the supervisory powers of the regulators, the Authority for the Financial Markets (**AFM**) and the Dutch Central Bank (**DNB**), are subject to the General Administrative Law Act (**GALA**) (see No 16).
- Breaches of certain provisions of the FSA are sanctionable under criminal law under the Economic Offences Act (**EOA**).
- Resolutions that are adopted on the basis of voting rights attached to an interest in an undertaking (Art. 2:118/228 of the Dutch Civil Code (**DCC**)) obtained without the required declaration of no objection may be annulled (Art. 3:104(2) FSA).

2 Origin

Reason for the supervision of financial markets

On 27 July 1914, as a result of the impending First World War, a steep fall in prices on the Amsterdam stock exchanges took place. Subsequently, major lenders withdrew their loans. The fall in the prices of collateralised securities caused a concern that lenders would disadvantage their borrowers if those securities were sold under execution at lower prices. Two days later, the stock market closed to prevent a collapse.

This was the reason for the first supervisory law act in the Netherlands, the Stock Exchange Act 1914.

The Stock Exchange Act 1914 contained a scheme to protect borrowers against execution (by lenders). In response to the criticism from the major lenders that this law restricted their right of execution, the legislator stated: '*in such a serious crisis, protection does not apply to the "large ones" but to the "small ones"*'. This statement is a good reflection of the background of financial supervision.

The government left the practical organisation and the stock market supervision to the Dutch Stock Exchange Association; de facto self-regulation in addition to the more formal supervision of the government.

Further development

Influenced by European regulations and abuses, the government increasingly interfered with the stock market and securities trading from the 1980s onwards, as is evidenced by the following:

- In 1985 this development led to the Securities Transactions Act (**STA**), which focused on the regulation of off-exchange trading.
- In 1990, the Investment Institutions (Supervision) Act (**IISA**) replaced the provisions of the STA rules that related to investments funds.
- In 1991, the Disclosure of Major Holdings in Listed Companies Act (**DMHLCA**) set rules regarding the disclosure of control or an interest in listed companies.
- In 1992, the STA and the Stock Exchange Act 1914 were replaced by the Securities Transactions (Supervision) Act (**STSA**) which emphasised that the government has a responsibility for the adequate functioning of the securities markets, given their growing importance for the economy.

Non-investment-related supervision

Supervisory law also developed in other areas, including the following:

- **Banking**: the first supervision took place on the basis of one article in the Bank Act 1948. This statutory supervisory regime developed from the Credit System (Supervision) Act 1952, via the Credit System (Supervision) Act 1978, to the Credit System (Supervision) Act 1992 (**CSSA 1992**).
- **Insurance**: the supervision of life insurers originally took place under the Royal Decree of 1830, which expired in 1880. From 1923, the Life Insurance Act applied, and for non-life insurers, from 1961 the Non-life Insurance Act. Both were replaced in 1987 by the Insurance Industry (Supervision) Act, which in turn was replaced in 1994 by the Insurance Industry (Supervision) Act 1993 (**IIA 1993**).
- **Consumer credit**: the first provisions under public law were included in the 1936 Act on the repayment undertaking, which

was replaced in 1964 by the Instalment Credit Sales Act. A second law that was aimed at consumer protection was the Consumer Money Credit Act (replacing the 1932 Moneylenders Act). Both were (partially) merged into the Consumer Credit Act 1992 (CCA). This in turn was merged in 2006 with the Insurance Brokerage Business Act into the Financial Services Provision Act (**FSPA**).

Tilting from sectoral supervision to functional supervision

Until 2002, financial supervision in the Netherlands was of a sectoral nature; each sector had its own law and its own supervisor (see Table 1).

Table 1 Sectoral financial monitoring

Sector	Law	Regulator
Investment firms (at that time still referred to as 'securities institutions')	STSA	Securities Board of the Netherlands (**STE**, later the AFM)
AIFs	IISA	STE
Banks	CSSA 1992	DNB
Life and non-life insurers	IIA 1993	Pension and Insurance Supervisory Authority of the Netherlands (**PVK**, later merged into DNB)
Funeral expenses and benefits in kind insurers	Insurance Supervision (Benefits in Kind for Funerals) Act	PVK
Financial service providers (e.g. consumer lenders and insurance intermediaries)	FSPA	STE
Listed companies	DMHLCA	STE

This classification proved to be impractical as the boundaries between financial companies and products blurred increasingly, because:

- certain financial firms developed into financial conglomerates with activities in various segments of the financial sector (banking market, insurance market, investment market, etc.); and
- an increasing number of products appeared with a cross-sectoral market character such as the investment mortgage and annuity policies with an investment element.

This prompted the legislator to 'tilt' the supervisory model in 2002, from the sectoral supervisory model to the functional supervisory model (also referred to as the *'twin peaks' model*). Under this model, DNB is responsible for the prudential supervision of all financial firms, while the AFM is responsible for the conduct of business supervision of all financial firms (see No 3).

In 2007, the financial supervision laws were aligned with the functional supervisory model. These financial supervisory laws were transposed into a single law, the FSA.

Further developments

The FSA constantly adapts to:

- address incidents;
- stay in line with the developing financial markets; and
- implement new and amended European directives (see No 4).

3 Objectives (prudential and conduct of business supervision)

The FSA lays down the rules for prudential and conduct of business supervision, from which the objectives of the FSA are derived. Both types of supervision together concern the protection of procurers of financial services, such as investors, savers and policyholders.

Prudential supervision

Prudential supervision focuses on the soundness of financial firms and the stability of the financial system (Art. 1:24 FSA, see Nos 38-56).

- **Micro-prudential supervision**: regards the financial health of an undertaking, taking into account whether the undertaking has sufficient capital buffers to absorb potential losses.
- **Macro-prudential supervision**: regards the interaction between financial firms and their environment (other financial firms, financial markets, infrastructure and the real economy).

Conduct of business supervision

Conduct of business supervision focuses on fair and transparent financial market processes, balanced relationships between market parties and careful treatment of clients (Art. 1:25 FSA, see Nos 63-78).

This type of supervision also regards settling information asymmetry between providers of financial services and products and their customers, as well as between those customers.

4 European influences

European law

On the one hand, the FSA consists of national rules. On the other hand, the FSA consists of the implementation of a large number of European directives. The most well-known directives are:

- Alternative Investment Fund Managers Directive (2011/61/EU, **AIFMD**) with regard to AIFMs;
- Undertakings for Collective Investment in Transferable Securities Directive (2009/65/EC, **UCITS Directive**) regarding UCITS;
- Capital Requirements Directive (2013/36/EU, **CRD**) regarding capital requirements for Banks and Investment Firms;
- Markets in Financial Instruments Directive (2014/65/EU, **MiFID**) regarding investment firms, trading venues and data reporting service providers;
- Solvency II Directive regarding insurers (2009/138/EU);
- Transparency Directive (2004/109/EC) regarding holdings in issuers; and
- Payment Services Directive (2015/2366/EU).

Financial Services Action Plan

In 1999, the European Commission (**EC**) published the Financial Services Action Plan (**FSAP**) which proposed policy objectives and concrete measures to improve the single market for financial services by 2005.

The FSAP proposed priorities and a timetable for the implementation of 42 specific measures (*i.e.* directives and regulations). In doing so, three strategic objectives were pursued:

- the creation of a wholesale internal market (business market) for financial services;
- the creation of open and secure retail markets (private market); and
- the strengthening of the rules on prudential supervision.

Lamfalussy legislative procedure

Given the size of the FSAP, a legislative methodology (also known as the Lamfalussy procedure) was designed in 2001 to improve the quality and effectiveness of European legislation and regulation in the financial sector. This procedure consists of the following four 'levels' of regulation:

- **Level 1 – Framework legislation**: after consultation with the parties concerned, the EC makes a legislative proposal for framework legislation in the form of directives or regulations. This framework legislation must be adopted by the European Parliament and the Council under the 'ordinary legislative procedure'.
- **Level 2 – Regulatory or implementing technical standards**: the EC, in cooperation with the European Financial Supervisors (see below), drafts a proposal for regulatory technical standards or implementing standards to further flesh out the level 1 legislation. In practice financial supervisors are leading and the EC adopts their proposals.
- **Level 3 – Guidelines and recommendations**: the European financial supervisors translate legislation that is not already covered by regulatory or implementing technical standards into guidelines and recommendations. This will ensure a uniform and consistent application of the new legislation within all member states.

- **Level 4 – Control**: after the directive or regulation has been introduced, the EC must check whether it has been implemented in national law by the member states in a timely and correct manner and identify differences in impact at the national level. In the exceptional case where the EC finds that a member state has implemented a directive or regulation incompletely or incorrectly, or has not amended conflicting national laws, it may bring an action before the Court of Justice.

Capital Markets Union

The Capital Markets Union (**CMU**) is a plan of the EC to mobilise capital in the EU. The CMU should make it easier for savers and investors to invest cross-border and to raise capital without banks. In this way, the EC also aims to stimulate economic growth. Introduced in 2015, the plan has already led to several regulatory initiatives, *e.g.*:

- Sustainable Finance Action Plan;
- SME Growth Market; and
- Fintech Action Plan;

and reforms relating to:

- corporate bonds;
- crowdfunding; and
- retail investment products.

Mutual recognition

In the EU, a system of mutual recognition applies, which involves the principle of 'home state control'. This means that member states recognise each other's supervision as equivalent to their own, because this supervision is based on the same European rules. Therefore, an authorisation obtained in one member state is considered sufficient to carry out activities in all other member states. As such, the European licence functions as a 'European passport' in the rest of the EU (and Norway, Iceland and Liechtenstein) (see Nos 25 and 37).

Brexit

On 23 June 2016, the people of the United Kingdom voted to leave the EU in a referendum. Since then, much has happened politically. Currently, the situation is still uncertain and the preconditions that are going to apply, at the time of writing this book, are still unclear. It may be possible that the United Kingdom will be classified as a third country for the provision of financial services in Europe, which will significantly change the provision of services to and from the United Kingdom. For example, it may not be possible to use the European passport and financial service providers based in the United Kingdom may no longer be bound by European rules. From a regulatory perspective, this is already being anticipated in the Netherlands, see *e.g.* the (temporary) Art. 10 Exemption (No 35), but what the ultimate effect of Brexit on the European financial market will be remains to be seen.

European financial regulators

The financial crisis of 2007 revealed major gaps in the European framework for the supervision of the international financial system. In 2008, the EC commissioned the de Larosière Group to make recommendations to strengthen the financial supervision in Europe. In 2009, the de Larosière report was published. The core of the report concerns the design of European supervision. Additionally, the report contains important recommendations for strengthening and, where necessary, harmonising regulations within Europe.

A recommendation from the de Larosière report formed the basis for the establishment of three European Supervisory Authorities (**ESAs**):

- European Banking Authority (**EBA**);
- European Insurance and Occupational Pensions Authority (**EIOPA**); and
- European Securities and Markets Authority (**ESMA**).

These European regulators:

- consist of the relevant national supervisors of all member states;
- have the power to set binding standards, and play an important role in the regulatory process at a European level (see above); and
- do not carry out formal supervision, which is carried out at a national level.

Maximum harmonisation

Nowadays, most directives prescribe maximum harmonisation: the Dutch legislator is then obliged to implement European directives, without too many deviations, in the Dutch FSA. Regulations have direct effect in the member states and are therefore not transposed into national rules. Examples are the MiFIR (Regulation (EU) No 600/2014) and the Prospectus Regulation (see No 79).

By legislating through regulations more frequently, the aim is to create a Single Rulebook. The Single Rulebook was also introduced in the de Larosière report and forms the backbone of the banking union and of the regulation of the EU's financial sector in general. The core objectives of the Single Rulebook are:

- eliminating legislative differences between member states;

- ensuring the same level of consumer protection; and
- creating a level playing field for banks across the EU.

5 Structure

The FSA has a layered structure with two levels of legislation.

Level of legislation

The FSA itself is the first level of legislation in which a large number of provisions provide for further elaboration by a general administrative measure (**gam**) (see *e.g.* Art. 4:16(3) FSA). The FSA consists of eight parts in which a wide range of subjects are dealt with. The main elements of these parts are as follows:

- **General part** (Part 1) contains:
  - definitions of terms used in the various parts (see Nos 6 to 13);
  - scoping provisions (see No 14);
  - affectability of legal acts (see No 15);
  - provisions for supervisors, on cooperation with other supervisors, their powers of enforcement, confidentiality, liability and publication possibilities (see Nos 16-19);
  - procedural provisions (see No 20); and
  - remuneration rules (see No 21).
- **Part Market access for financial firms** (Part 2) contains:
  - activities subject to authorisation (see Nos 26 to 35);
  - licensing requirements (see No 36); and
  - possibilities to carry out activities from the Netherlands in other jurisdictions (see No 37).
- **Part Prudential supervision of financial firms** (Part 3) contains:

- a statutory exemption to the banking licence obligation for group finance companies (see No 39);
- prohibitions regarding obtaining repayable funds and the use of the word 'bank' (see Nos 40 and 41);
- rules on suitability, trustworthiness, integrity and structuring and design (see Nos 42-44);
- rules of a prudential nature, including those relating to minimum capital, solvency, liquidity and technical provisions (see Nos 45 to 49);
- the regime regarding qualifying holdings in certain financial firms (see No 50); and
- special measures for financial firms, including those relating to portfolio transfers, capital add-ons, recovery plans, short-term financial plans, the investor-compensation scheme, the deposit guarantee scheme, investment policy principles and investment policy, and provisions regarding guideline group supervision (see Nos 51-56).

- **Part Special measures and facilities relating to financial firms** (Part 3A) contains:
  - rules relating to the resolution of banks, certain investment firms and insurers (see Nos 57-62).
- **Part Conduct of business supervision of financial firms** (Part 4) contains:
  - rules on suitability, professional competence, reliability and integrity (see Nos 64-67);
  - rules for the organisation of certain financial firms (see No 68);
  - rules on customer handling (see Nos 69-71); and
  - additional rules per type of financial firm for organisation and customer handling (see Nos 73-77).

- **Part Conduct of business supervision of the financial market** (Part 5) contains:
  - rules for access to the Dutch markets for market operators and for managing a regulated market (see No 81);
  - control and capital interest in issuers, market abuse (see Nos 82 and 83);
  - securities-related market conduct of business supervision (see No 84); and
  - public offers of securities (see No 85).
- **Part Special measures relating to stability of the financial system** (Part 6) contains:
  - rules governing the expropriation of financial firms (see No 87).
- **Part Final provisions** (Part 7) contains:
  - certain administrative provisions.

In addition, the FSA contains annexes containing lists of:
- the classes of business in which the activity of a life insurer and of a non-life insurer are distinguished; and
- the articles of which a breach can lead to a fine or an order subject to a penalty (see No 16).

Lower regulation

The second level of legislation is intended to further elaborate the law and consists of:
- implementing decrees (gams);
- ministerial regulations; and
- regulators' rules.

The most commonly used of these are:
- **Implementing decrees**

- Definitions (FSA) Decree (**DD**);
- Provisions on Scope (FSA) Decree (**PSFD**);
- EU Financial Markets Regulations (Implementation) Decree (**EU FMRD**);
- Financial Supervision (Funding) Decree 2019 (**FSD 2019**);
- Administrative Fines (Financial Sector) Decree (**AFD**);
- Market Access for Financial Undertakings (FSA) Decree (**MAFUD**);
- Prudential Rules (FSA) Decree (**PRD**);
- Special Prudential Measures, Investor Compensation and Deposit Guarantees (**FSA**) Decree (**SPMD**);
- Prudential Supervision of Financial Undertakings (FSA) Decree (**PSFUD**);
- Market Conduct Supervision (Financial Institutions) Decree (**MCSD**);
- Regulated Market (FSA) Decree (**RMD**);
- Disclosure of Major Holdings and Capital Interests in Securities-Issuing Institutions Decree (**DMHD**);
- Public Takeover Bids (FSA) Decree (**PTBD**);
- Market Abuse (FSA) Decree (**MAD**);
- Transparency of Securities-Issuing Institutions Decree (**TSID**);
- Takeover Bids Exemption Decree (**TBED**);
- Restrictions on Introducing into the Market, Distributing or Selling CFD's Decree (**RCFDD**); and
- Basel 2 Capital Accord (Implementation) Decree (**BCAD**).

- **Ministerial regulations**
  - FSA Implementing Regulations (**IR FSA**);
  - Performance of Duties Cross-border Cooperation Financial Supervisors (FSA) Regulation (**PDCR**);
  - Designated States (FSA) Decree (**DSD**);

- Exemption Regulation FSA;
- Financial Sector (Oath or Solemn Declaration) Regulation 2015 (**FSR 2015**);
- Exit qualifications and exam qualifications financial services (FSA) Regulation (**EEQR**); and
- Employees Investment Firms (Professional Competence) Regulation 2012 (**EIFR 2012**).

- **Regulators' rules**
  - Further Regulations on the Supervision of the Conduct of Financial Undertakings (FSA) (**FRSCFU**);
  - Numbered Accounts (FSA) Regulation (**NAR**);
  - Restrained Remuneration Policy Regulations (FSA) 2017 (**RRPR 2017**);
  - Specific Provisions CRD and CRR Regulation (**SPR**);
  - Statements from Financial Undertakings (FSA) Regulation 2011 (**SFUR 2011**); and
  - Prudential Supervision of Financial Groups (FSA) Regulation (**PSFGR**).

This is schematically visualised in Table 2.

Policy Rule

Finally, there are policy regulations of the regulators, including the:

- Policy Rule Tradability;
- Policy Rule Offering AIFs or UCITS under different names;
- Policy Rule Being active in the Netherlands Regulation 2013;
- Policy Rule Information Provision;
- Policy Rule Definition and Calculations of a Short-position within the meaning of the FSA;
- Policy Rule Suitability 2012;
- Policy Rule Scope and Execution Deposit Guarantee Scheme;

- Policy Rule Application European Supervisory Authorities (FSA);
- Policy Rule Notification Form Transactions in Financial Instruments within the Issuing Institution;
- Policy Rule ICAAP Investment Firms and AIFs (FSA) 2015; and
- Policy Rule Maximising ratio deposits and investment (FSA).

This Boom Basics FSA will follow the same order of topics as the FSA. As has become clear from the above, much of financial supervision today is set out in regulations (see No 4). Some of these regulations are discussed in this Boom Basics FSA (see Nos 79 and 83). For a more complete picture, reference is also made to regulations in this Boom Basics FSA in some places as well.

Table 2 Layered structure FSA

Part 1	Part 2	Part 3	Part 3A	Part 4	Part 5	Part 6	Part 7
General provisions	Market access to financial institutions	Prudential supervision of financial companies	Special measures and provisions concerning financial firms	Conduct of business supervision of financial firms	Conduct of business supervision of financial markets	Special measures relating to the stability of the financial system	Final provisions
- DD - PSFD - EU FMRD - FSD 2019 - AFD - PDCR - RRPR 2017 - RCFDD	- MAFUD - DSD	- PRD - SPMD - PFSUD - FSR 2015 - BCAD		- MCSD - FSR 2015 - EEQR - EIFR 2012	-DMHD -PTBD -MAD -TSID -TBED		
	Exemption Regulation FSA			Exemption Regulation FSA			
IR FSA		IR FSA		IR FSA			
		- NAR - SPR - PSFGR - SFUR 2011		FRSCFU			

II General part (Part 1)

6 Definitions

In many provisions of the FSA defined terms are used, primarily in the prohibitory provisions (see Nos 26-35). Art. 1:1 FSA contains the general definitions of terms used in all Parts of the FSA.

For example:
Art. 2:65 FSA prohibits the management of an AIF and the offering of units in an AIF. Art. 1:1 FSA contains the definitions of the terms in bold.

Below, we discuss several important basic terms of the FSA that may seem to have similar meanings and therefore are easy to confuse with each other (Nos 7-11). We conclude with two important terms: 'offering' and 'in the course of a profession or business' (see No 13).

7 Financial product, financial instrument and security

Financial products form the largest subset and include financial instruments, which in its turn include securities. By way of illustration: some of the prohibitory provisions refer to financial products, but exclude financial instruments.

For example:
It is prohibited to advise on financial products other than financial instruments (Art. 2:75 FSA).

Financial product

The following is considered to be a financial product:

- an investment object;
- a payment account, including the related payment facilities;
- electronic money;
- a financial instrument;
- credit;
- a savings account, including the related savings facilities;
- an insurance that is not reinsurance;
- a premium pension claim; or
- any other product that is designated as such by a general administrative measure.

Financial instrument

This term follows from MiFID and therefore is relevant in the context of investment services, investment activities, regulated markets and multilateral trading facilities (see No 10).

The following is considered as a financial instrument:

- **a security**;
  This definition is discussed at the end of this paragraph.
- **a money-market instrument**;
  These are instruments that are usually traded on the money market, such as treasury bills, certificates of deposit and commercial papers.
- **a unit in an AIF or UCITS, not being a security**;
  These are participations or shares in:
  - an open-ended AIF or UCITS; or
  - a closed-end AIF or UCITS which are not tradeable (and therefore do not qualify as a 'security').

  See No 10 for a description of the terms 'open-end' and 'closed-end'.

- **a forward agreement, future, interest rate forward agreement and contracts for difference;**
  - A forward agreement involves the obligation (not the right) to buy or sell a certain quantity of a certain underlying asset (such as currency, goods or commodities) at a specified price and with delivery at a specified point in the future.
  - *Futures* are standardised forward agreements and are traded on a regulated market.
  - *Forwards* are non-standardised forward agreements and are traded privately.
- **a commodity derivative;**

  These are derivatives of raw materials such as metal, gold, land, agricultural products and electricity. A distinction is made between:
  - an issued tradeable instrument relating to a commodity or commodity derivative that has the characteristics of other derivative financial instruments and is settled in cash;
  - commodity derivatives that are settled in cash;
  - commodity derivatives that are physically settled and traded on a regulated market or MTF;
  - commodity derivatives that have the characteristics of other derivative financial instruments that are physically settled and are not for commercial purposes; and
  - commodity derivatives that have the characteristics of other derivative financial instruments and which are settled in cash.
- **an option;**

  An option gives the buyer the right to buy (call option) or sell (put option) a fixed quantity of securities or other goods at a certain price at a time in the future. The seller of the option (also known as the writer of the option) is, in return for his right to receive a premium from the buyer, obliged to sell (put option) or buy (call option) the securities or other goods if the buyer exercises its option.

- **a swap; and**
  A swap is a reciprocal agreement aimed at periodically swapping or exchanging certain values, *e.g.* different interest rates (interest rate swap) or different currencies (swap).
- **a greenhouse gas emission allowance.**
  A greenhouse gas emission allowance gives the right to emit a certain amount of greenhouse gases or other harmful gases. The total number of available allowances is limited but they can be traded freely at an auction.

Security

This term follows from the Prospectus Regulation (see No 79). The following is considered a security:

- a tradeable share or a similar tradeable instrument or right (including units in a closed-end AIF);
- a tradable bond or other tradable debt instrument; and
- any other tradable instrument issued by a legal entity, undertaking or institution by which a security referred to in (a) or (b) can be acquired by exercising the rights attached to it or by conversion, or which can be settled in cash, such as convertible bonds or warrants.

Typical for all types of securities is the element of tradability. The AFM's Policy Rule Tradability states that this element concerns '*all constructions in which an instrument can be transferred indirectly or immediately*'.

8 *Customer, consumer and public*

The legislator intends to 'protect' certain counterparties as procurers of financial services and financial products. They are referred to in different ways, depending on the context.

Client

This term is used in the context of insurance and investment services. It is no longer defined in the FSA because it has the same meaning as in ordinary speech and therefore sees upon both the consumer and the business procurer.

Consumer

This term is used in the context of certain financial products (mainly credit) and means '*a natural person who is not acting in the course of a business or profession*'.

For example:
If a natural person takes out a credit to finance his sole proprietorship (not a consumer) or to finance his house (consumer).

Public

This term is used for the definition of 'bank' and for the prohibition to obtain repayable funds (Art. 3:5 FSA) (see No 40). However, it is not (yet) defined in the FSA. The legislator has confirmed that, until further notice, this term may be interpreted as the pair of terms 'beyond a closed circle and from others than PMPs'. For the definition of PMPs see No 9.

A closed circle is a circle consisting of persons or companies from which a party obtains repayable funds, whereby the following conditions are met:

- the circle is accurately defined;
- the access criteria are defined beforehand, are verifiable and do not facilitate simple entry of persons or companies not belonging to the circle; and
- the members of the circle have an existing legal relationship with the party obtaining the repayable funds at the time such funds are obtained, on the basis of which such members may reasonably be aware of the financial situation of such party.

For example:
Employees of an employer, group companies and family members.

9 Professional market party, professional investor, eligible counterparty, qualified investor and institutional investor

Certain parties are considered experts in financial services and financial products, which is why dealing with them is not or less regulated in the FSA. Professional market parties constitute the largest subset and include qualified investors who in turn include professional investors.

Professional market party

Although this term is defined in Art. 1:1 FSA, it is no longer used officially in the FSA. However, it is used unofficially in the definition of 'bank' and the prohibition of obtaining repayable funds (Art. 3:5

FSA) (see No 40). The following is considered as a 'Professional Market Party' (**PMP**):

- a qualified investor or the subsidiary of a qualified investor that is subjected to the supervision of the qualified investor on a consolidated basis; or
- any other person or partnership designates as Professional Market Party in Art. 3 DD.

For example:
It follows from Art. 3 DD that a person from whom repayable funds are attracted qualifies as PMP if the amount of such repayable funds is at least € 100,000.

Professional investor and 'eligible counterparty'

This term is relevant for the applicability of certain conduct of business rules for investment services (see No 70). The following parties are considered 'professional investors':

- a bank*;
- an AIFM*;
- a management undertaking of a pension fund or of a comparable legal entity or undertaking (*e.g.* a general insurance undertaking);
- an AIF*;
- an investment firm*;
- a national or regional government body, or government body administering the public debt*;
- a central bank*;
- a financial institution*;
- an international or supranational organisation governed by public law or comparable international organisation*;
- a pension fund or comparable legal entity or undertaking*;

- an undertaking whose main activity is investing in financial instruments, implementing securitisation programmes or other financial transactions;
- a legal entity or an undertaking that satisfies two of the following size requirements:
  - a balance sheet total of at least € 20,000,000;
  - a net turnover of at least € 40,000,000; and
  - equity capital of at least € 2,000,000; or
- an insurer*.

The parties marked with an asterisk also qualify as an 'eligible counterparty'.

As follows from the definition, it is possible for a non-professional investor to be qualified, upon request, as a professional investor (opt-up) and vice versa: a professional investor can be qualified as a non-professional investor (opt-down) or an eligible counterparty (opt-up). See No 70 for an explanation.

Qualified investor

This term is, among other things, relevant for an exemption to the obligation to publish a prospectus (Art. 3 Prospectus Regulation) (see No 79). The following parties are considered a 'qualified investor':

- a professional investor, unless it requested to be treated as a non-professional investor;
- a person who, upon request, is treated as a professional investor; or
- an eligible counterparty, unless it requested to be treated as a non-professional investor.

In fact, this definition is identical to the aggregate of the definitions of 'professional investor' and 'eligible counterparty'.

Institutional investor

This term is relevant for the applicability of certain conduct of business rules with respect to voting on shares (see No 86). The following parties are considered 'institutional investors':

- an AIF;
- a UCITS;
- a life insurer;
- a pension fund; or
- a premium pension institution (**PPI**).

10 *AIF, undertaking for the collective investment in transferable securities (UCITS), investment fund, investment company and investment firm*

AIF

For the definition of 'AIF', the FSA refers to (Art. 4(1)(a)) AIFMD: '*a collective investment undertaking, including investment compartments thereof, which raises capital from a number of investors, with a view to investing it in accordance with a defined investment policy for the benefit of those investors*'.

The following elements are important:

- **collectivity**: this is the case if the return on an investment accrues to several investors (participants). This is an important difference compared to individual asset management;
- **a number of investors**: this may be the case, even if there is only one investor, if the goal is to attract multiple participants;

- **raising capital**: in principle, this covers all goods and property rights (often money, but also other goods may be contributed) which the AIF receives from participants; and
- **investing in accordance with a defined investment policy**: this concerns the policy on how the raised capital is invested in order to generate a return for investors. In this respect, the distinction with entrepreneurship is particularly relevant (and not always clear in practice).

ESMA distinguishes between an undertaking pursuing an investment objective and an undertaking having a general commercial or industrial objective. The AFM indicated that the expired Policy Rule on undertaking and investing still contains relevant indicators for determining whether entrepreneurship or investing is involved.

Open-end and closed-end

The FSA distinguishes between open-end and closed-end AIFs. These terms are not defined in the FSA.

- It follows from Art. 2(p) of the Prospectus Regulation that an AIF other than the closed-end type, and therefore open-ended, is *an AIF of which the units are, at the holder's request, repurchased or redeemed, directly or indirectly, out of its assets.*
- Therefore, a closed-end AIF is *an AIF of which units are not repurchased or redeemed early.*

This distinction is relevant for the licence obligation of the manager and the prospectus obligation (see Nos 32 and 79).

Undertakings for collective investment in transferable securities (UCITS)

The rules for UCITS follow from the UCITS Directive. A UCITS is an open-ended investment institution which sole goal is the collective investment in transferable securities. The main distinction between a UCITS and an AIF is that a UCITS invests in compliance with certain investment restrictions and diversification requirements. As a rule of thumb, a UCITS must invest in transferable securities or certain other financial instruments, and not in real estate or other goods.

Investment fund or investment company

AIFs and UCITS may take the form of an investment company or an investment fund. The difference is that an investment company has legal personality and an investment fund does not.

Investment firm

An investment firm provides investment services or performs investment activities.

- Under '**the provision of an investment service**' is understood:
  - *the reception and transmission of orders from clients in relation to financial instruments in the course of a profession or business;*
  - *the execution of orders on behalf of those clients in relation to financial instruments in the course of a profession or business;*

    These two investment services are also being referred to as execution-only services. This means that the investor makes his investment decisions independently and the investment firms only orders the purchase (order) of a financial instrument. These services are subject to a limited set of conduct of business rules (see No 70).
  - *Individual portfolio management;*

Individual portfolio management is defined as '*the discretionary management of financial instruments belonging to one person*'. The words 'on a discretionary basis' mean that an investor leaves the making of investment decisions to the investment firm (on the basis of agreements made with the investor).

Individual portfolio must be distinguished from collective portfolio management by managers of AIFs and UCITS.

- *the provision of advice relating to financial instruments in the course of a profession or business; or*

  Advising is recommending one or more specific financial instruments to a specific client. The concept of 'investment advice' is further elaborated as the provision of 'personalised' recommendations to a client in respect of one or more transactions in financial instruments (Art. 9 of the MiFID Delegated Regulation). Therefore, general advice that is not tailored to the personal characteristics or circumstances of the client does not amount to investment advice.
- *the underwriting and / or placing of financial instruments upon their offering (as referred to in the Prospectus Regulation) in the course of a profession or business as referred to in the Prospectus Regulation on a commitment basis and the placing of financial instruments upon their offering (as referred to in the Prospectus Regulation) in the course of a profession or business without a commitment basis.*

  When issuing financial instruments (e.g. shares), the issuer often engages a third party to 'place' such instruments with investors. If this third party and the issuer agreed that it will purchase financial instruments that are not placed with investors, this amounts to placing on a commitment basis.

- The term '**performance of investment activities**' refers to:

- *dealing on own account in the course of a profession or business ('proprietary trading').*
  Dealing on own account is trading in financial instruments with the firm's own capital, rather than dealing for a client. This is often done by market makers. Market makers continuously quote buy and sell prices, against which investors can trade;
- *the operation of an organised trading facility in the course of a profession or business; or*
- *the operation of a multilateral trading facility in the course of a profession or business.*

Orders in financial instruments can be executed on different trading platforms:

- a regulated market (in daily speech: the stock exchange);
- an organised trading facility (**OTF**); and
- a multilateral trading Facility (**MTF**),

but also with an investment firm that applies systematic internalisation (**SI**).

The definitions of regulated market and MTF are very similar. Both are platforms where third parties' buying and selling intentions in relation to financial instruments are brought together.

Regulated markets are regulated in Part 5 and MTFs in Part 4. The difference between the definition of a regulated market and a MTF in Art. 1:1 FSA is that financial instruments must comply with certain rules in order to be admitted for trading on a regulated market. The definition of MTF does not include such requirement, but this does not change the fact that the MTF may impose similar rules. An OTF is a multilateral system, not being a regulated market or a MTF, which brings together third parties' buying and selling intentions in relation to bonds, structured finance products, emission allowances and derivatives, as a result of which an agreement is concluded.

An investment firm that applies SI settles clients' buying and selling orders against its own accounts. Since the investment firm itself is the counterparty of its clients, it deals on its own account and simultaneously executes client orders. Basically, it matches its own trading book with the demand and supply of its clients.

11 *Financial firm, financial institution and financial service provider*

Financial firm

This term covers all firms to which the ongoing supervisory requirements of Part 3 and Part 4 may apply, regardless of whether they are profit-making or not (Art. 1:3 FSA). These are, in addition to the licence holders (see No 22), with the exception of electronic money institutions (but that seems to be an erratum):

- AIFs;
- UCITS; and
- pension custodians (see *e.g.* Art. 3:53 FSA and Art. 4:9 FSA).

Financial institution

This term refers to those who, while not being a bank, mainly:

- carry out one or more of the activities, referred to in points 2 to 12 and 15 in Annex I to CRD; or
- acquire or hold participations.

The first category regards subsidiaries of licensed banks, which carry out certain banking activities (with the exception of obtaining deposits or other repayable funds). If such financial institution holds a declaration of supervision by DNB, it may perform these activities in other member states (Art. 3:110 FSA in conjunction with Art. 2:112 FSA and Art. 2:114 FSA). Only in those circumstances, the FSA is relevant for a financial institution having its seat in the Netherlands (Art. 3:110 para. 6 FSA) and can it be regarded as a financial firm.

The second category regards parent companies of banks (and investment firms) and is only relevant for the definition of 'financial holding' and therefore for group supervision (see No 56).

Financial services provider

This term refers to those who:

- offer a financial product other than a financial instrument (*e.g.* a lender or provider of investment objects);
- advise on a financial product other than a financial instrument (a consultant);
- intermediate (*e.g.* an insurance intermediary);
- intermediate in reinsurances;
- act as an authorised agent; or
- act as a subauthorised agent.

This definition is required to bring this otherwise unmentioned and very diverse category of service providers within the scope of the term 'financial firm'.

12 *Key information document and key investor information document*

When providing a financial service and offering financial products to retail investors, typically an information document must be provided. This serves to protect the retail investor and ensures that he can make an informed decision whether to invest. There are various information documents which, although similar, impose different requirements. In addition to the key information document (**KID**) and the key investor information document (**KIID**), the requirement to publish a prospectus exists when securities are offered to the public or admitted to trading on a regulated market (see No 79).

Key information document

For a large number of investment products and insurance products with an investment component (*i.e.*packaged retail and insurance-based investment products) a KID must be provided.

This follows from the PRIIPs Regulation (Regulation (EU) No 1286/2014, **PRIIPs Regulation**). Examples are investment funds, investment objects, structured products and derivatives. The KID consists of a maximum of three pages and provides insight into the operation, risks, costs and return of the relevant investment product. This information is also subject to requirements. For example, information on risks should be included by way of a risk indicator, whereas information on the expected return must be displayed by means of performance scenarios. In the Delegated PRIIPs Regulation (Regulation (EU) No 2017/653), the requirements for a KID are set out in more detail. By using the KID, retail investors are enabled to easily compare various providers and different products.

Key investor information

AIFMs and UCITS management companies are required to draw up a KIID in relation to the investment funds they manage. This obligation follows from the UCITS Directive. The KIID consists of a maximum of two pages and provides insight into the investment policy, past performance, the nature and risks of the investment funds offered. The KIID must provide the retail investor with appropriate information to enable him to make a well-advised decision before investing in a particular investment fund. With respect to AIFs and UCITS that, in addition to the requirement to disclose a KIID, are subject to the requirement to disclose a KID, a temporary exemption applies until 31 December 2021 in relation to the requirement to disclose a KID.

13 Offering and 'in the course of a profession or business'

Offering

The definition of offering is linked to the term 'offer' as referred to in Art. 6:217 DCC which is relevant to various prohibitions in Part 2 and contains four different elements. Offering entails the following:

- *in the course of a profession* directly or indirectly making a sufficiently defined proposal to enter into an agreement as a counterparty:
  - with a consumer in relation to a financial product (not being a financial instrument, premium pension claim or insurance);
  - as a result of which a premium pension claim arises;
  - in relation to an insurance; or

- directly or indirectly making a sufficiently determined proposal to enter into an agreement, as counterparty, relating to a unit in an AIF or a UCITS or relating to solicit or obtain, directly or indirectly, funds or other property from a client for the purpose of holding a unit in an AIF or a UCITS.

The entering into, management or execution of one of these three types of agreements in the course of a profession or business, and the offering of such agreements through an intermediary, also falls within scope of the definition.

In the course of a profession or business

Whether a certain action is performed in the 'course of a profession or business' is determined by examining if purpose of the business (*e.g.* according to the articles of association) is to provide the relevant financial services.

In other cases, it depends on the specific circumstances. Potential leads are:

- the way in which the person providing a financial service presents itself externally;
- the fact that the provision of financial services does not;
- only occur occasionally (but *e.g.* regularly and systematically); or
- the fact that the person providing the financial service receives a commission for the provision of such services (from the client himself or from a third party).

A financial service provided on an occasional basis in the context of another professional activity of the service provider, does not qualify as 'in the course of a profession or business'. Consequently, no licence is required. However, in such case it must concern activities that necessarily directly result from that other professional activity.

14 *Scoping provisions*

The scoping provisions determine for different parties or activities whether they are (partially) subject to the FSA. Such provisions may exclude or include parties or activities from the scope of application. Below, we discuss a selection and we mention some other scoping provisions in Nos 23 and 24.

Government-related institutions

The European Central Bank (**ECB**), DNB, the Agency of the Ministry of Finance, the Social Insurance Bank, the Employee Insurance Agency (**UWV**) and the Dutch Terrorism Risk Reinsurance Company are excluded from (parts of) the FSA (Arts. 1:2, 1:6 and 1:6a FSA).

Pension funds and their asset managers

Pension funds that conclude and settle insurances, without these activities being regarded as performed in the course of the business of life insurers or the business of non-life insurer (Art. 1:8 FSA), are exempt from the FSA.

From the FSA (except from Part 1 and Part 5) are also exempt:

- financial services (excluding the offering of units) that are provided by sectoral pension funds, company pension funds, company savings funds and occupational pension funds to the business sector, company or professional group which they are affiliated with (within the meaning of the Pension Act); and

- asset managers that manage the assets of pension funds to which they are affiliated (within the meaning of Art. 2:24b DCC) (Art. 1:15 FSA).

Online services

Financial services provided by an information society (online services such as internet banking and the offering of credit via internet) are excluded from the scope of the FSA if the relevant financial firm in question has:

- its seat; or
- in the case of a financial firm seated in a non-member state, a branch,

in another EU member state or a state that is a party to the Agreement on the European Economic Area (**EEA**) (Art. 1:16 FSA). This is based on the country of origin principle of the Electronic Commerce Directive (2000/31/EC).

Please note that the notification requirements do apply to insurers that have their seat in another member state and insurers with a branch in another member state that intend to carry out their business on a cross-border basis in the Netherlands (see Nos 25 *and* 37*).*

Reversely, such services do fall under the scope of the FSA if they are provided in another member state by a financial firm from within the Netherlands (Art. 1:17 FSA).

15 *Affectability of legal acts*

The FSA contains supervisory rules that are aimed at market participants. These rules also affect the legal relationships between such market participants and their clients, *e.g.* by the various duties on market participants to disclose information to clients. However, if a market participant performs a legal act that is in breach of the FSA (or underlying regulations or the TFEU, to the extent it does not imperatively provide otherwise), that legal act is in principle not void or voidable (Art. 1:23(1) and (2) FSA). Therefore, breaches of the supervisory rules do not have, in principle, consequences under civil law. However, this does not hold if the FSA explicitly provides otherwise, *e.g.* in Art. 4:74(4) FSA. This does not affect the fact that a legal act may be void or voidable on the basis of Art. 3:40(1) DCC, because it may be considered as contrary to public morality or public order. Additionally, other instruments under civil law may be available to the client, such as invoking error or an action arising from tort.

16 *Supervision and enforcement*

Financial supervision is a public function for which the Minister of Finance is responsible. This function is performed by the AFM and DNB, depending on which of them is the licensing authority for the specific financial firm. The ECB has a role in this function as well (see No 22).

The AFM and DNB have at their disposal various supervisory powers and enforcement instruments to monitor or enforce compliance with the FSA. These powers and instruments are laid down in the FSA and the GALA.

Supervisory powers

- Both (the administrative bodies and employees of) the AFM and DNB may **demand information** from anyone (Art. 1:74 FSA, respectively Art. 1:72 FSA in conjunction with Art. 5:11 GALA in conjunction with Art. 5:16 GALA).
- In addition, AFM's and DNB's employees are authorised **to enter** any premises (for entering a home, permission is required from the occupant, Art. 5:15 GALA), if necessary with the assistance of the police.
- It is also possible to demand **access** to business data and documents (Art. 5:17 GALA).

Duty to cooperate and principle of proportionality

- In principle, everyone is obliged to cooperate with, for example, a request for information (Art. 5:20 GALA).
- According to the principle of proportionality, the regulator must always be able to justify why exercising a specific supervisory power is 'reasonably necessary' in a specific case, and whether the exercise of this specific power is the least onerous (Art. 5:13 GALA).
- Furthermore, general principles of good governance are of relevance (Art. 3:1(2) GALA).

Enforcement powers

If the AFM or DNB ascertains that the FSA has been breached, they may take enforcement measures. They have at their disposal:

- remedial instruments: these are used to force ending the relevant breach; and

- punitive instruments: such as the administrative penalty (Art. 1:80 FSA).

In addition to the statutory enforcement instruments, the AFM and DNB also use more informal (i.e. not directly following from the FSA) enforcement measures, such as compliance briefings or written warnings (see the AFM 's and DNB's Enforcement Policy).

The most frequent remedial enforcement instruments are:
- the binding instruction (Art. 1:75 FSA, see also No 59);
- an order subject to a penalty (Art. 1:79 FSA);
- the undisclosed ('silent') administrator (Art. 1:76 FSA); and
- the withdrawal of the licence (Art. 1:104 FSA).

A binding instruction aims to ensure that a person follows a certain line of conduct, *e.g.*:
- to cease forbidden conduct;
- to modify the business operations in certain respects; or
- to 'release' a director or supervisory director of his or her duties because, according to the regulator, he or she is no longer suitable or trustworthy.

An order subject to a penalty is comparable to a binding instruction, with the difference that periodic penalties are incurred if the order is not complied with within the given period.

In exceptional situations, the regulator may appoint one or more persons as a (silent) administrator in a financial firm. Such appointment is not published. The tasks of the administrator should not be confused with those of a bankruptcy trustee, since his tasks are more similar to those of the trustee appointed under the law of persons and family law. The bodies and representatives of the financial firm require the prior approval of the administrator (after appointment) in order to exercise their powers.

As a last resort, a regulator may decide to withdraw a licence. Generally, the regulator will not exercise this instrument unless there are structural, serious shortcomings.

Administrative penalty

The purpose of an administrative penalty is to impact the offender financially. The FSA categorises penalties into three categories (Art. 1:81(2) FSA), each with a basis amount, a minimum amount and a maximum amount.

Table 3 Categories and amounts of penalties

Category	Basis amount	Minimum amount	Maximum amount
1	€ 10,000	€ 0	€ 10,000
2	€ 500,000	€ 0	€ 1,000,000
3	€ 2,500,000	€ 0	€ 5,000,000

The appendix to Art. 1:80 FSA contains the provisions of which a breach is penalisable. The applicability of a certain amount is set out in the AFD, in which each provision is included in a certain category.

The amount of the penalty may be increased or decreased depending on a number of variables, including:

- the seriousness and duration of the breach (Art. 1(b) AFD in conjunction with Art. 5:46(2) GALA);

- the culpability of the offender (Art. 2(3) AFD in conjunction with Art. 5:46(2) GALA); and
- its financial capacity (Art. 4 AFD in conjunction with Art. 5:46(2) GALA).

Furthermore, deviating (higher) penalties may be imposed on certain financial firms or for certain breaches, *e.g.* a certain percentage of the turnover or (at most) twice the benefit obtained from the relevant breach (Art. 1:81(3) FSA in conjunction with Art. 1:82 FSA).

New enforcement instruments

Influenced by European directives and regulations, the range of enforcement instruments has expanded in recent years, for example the power to suspend the exercise of voting rights (Art. 1:86 FSA) or to disqualify a person from its profession (Art. 1:87 FSA).

However, the regulators seem to be making little or no use of these new instruments so far.

17 Confidentiality and publication

Confidentiality

In principle, the AFM and DNB (and their employees) are subject to an obligation of confidentiality (Art. 1:89 FSA). A certain number of exhaustively defined statutory exemptions to this obligation of confidentiality exist. The AFM and DNB may disclose confidential information:

- between themselves (Art. 1:90 *et seq.* FSA), as further specified in the Cooperation Agreement 2016 between the AFM and DNB;

- to other European regulators and European authorities; and
- to the Dutch public prosecutor and the Dutch tax authorities.

The strict confidentiality regime of the regulators has been subject to discussion for some time. For example, both the AFM and DNB argued in favour of more transparency.

Disclosure

The AFM and DNB:

- may disclose public statements about certain breaches listed in Art. 1:94(1) FSA and the name of the offender (Art. 1:94(1) FSA);
- may disclose a public warning about every breach of the FSA and the name of the offender, if they believe that this is necessary to inform the public quickly and effectively in order to prevent or limit damages (Art. 1:94(2) FSA); and
- must disclose a decision to impose an administrative sanction (including the termination or restriction by the regulator of rights or powers as a result of a breach, and as the imposition of a prohibition) (Art. 1:97 FSA).

The applicable time limits for disclosure are:

- for an administrative fine for a 'serious' breach: as soon as possible (Art. 1:97(3) FSA);
- for an order subject to a penalty: as soon as possible after the penalty is incurred (Art. 1:97(4) FSA); and
- for other administrative sanctions: as soon as the relevant decision has become irrevocable (Art. 1:97(1) FSA).

Before the regulator proceeds with the disclosure of personally identifiable data a disclosure decision must be made (Art. 1:99(1) FSA). Such decision must specify the information to be disclosed, the manner of publication and the time limit within which such disclosure takes place. Subsequently, the disclosure may take place five business days following the date on which the party concerned has been notified of the disclosure decision (Art. 1:100(1) FSA). During such period, a request to suspend the disclosure may be submitted to the preliminary relief judge of the Court of Rotterdam (Art. 8:81 GALA). If such a request is made, the disclosure is automatically suspended until the preliminary relief judge has delivered its judgment (Art. 1:100(3) FSA). However, in the case of disclosure of statements (Art. 1:94(1) FSA), the personally identifiable data may only take place after the decision thereto has become irrevocable (Art. 1:100(2) FSA).

A shorter deadline (even 'immediately') applies if:

- protection of the interests that the FSA aims to protect does not allow any further delay; or
- the offender has publicly made available information about the breach or the decision to impose an administrative sanction to which the disclosure relates, and immediate disclosure is necessary in the public interest to protect the public confidence in the supervision of the financial markets (Art. 1:100a(1) FSA).

In principle, disclosure must always take place, but there may be reasons to do so on an anonymous basis. In this context, the regulator must conduct a (far-reaching) balancing of interests (Court of Rotterdam (interim relief judge) 29 September 2014, ECLI:RBROT:2014:8355).

18 *Liability of regulators*

A regulator may feel constrained to exercise its powers, because of potential liability. In order to remedy this problem, the AFM's and DNB's liability is limited to acts or omissions as a result of which the damage is significantly:

- caused by an intentional improper performance of a task or exercise of powers; or
- due to gross negligence (Art. 1:25d FSA).

This limitation of liability relates to acts of the regulators, their directors, members of their (supervisory) board and their employees, where such acts take place in the context of the performance of their statutory supervisory tasks under the FSA, but also to other laws under which they exercise supervision. Acts performed on the basis of the GALA also fall within scope of the limitation of liability, since such acts are directly related to the exercise of tasks and powers pursuant to the relevant supervisory rules.

The limitation of liability applies to:

- actual acts of the regulators, such as obtaining information or conducting investigations. For example, such acts may include sending a proposed decision to the party concerned to the wrong address; and
- legal acts performed by the regulators pursuant to the legal duties and powers conferred upon them by the relevant supervisory legislation, such as administrative decisions. Consequently, the limitation of liability also applies to the regulators' decisions that are nullified by the administrative court.

In order to fall within scope of the limitation of liability, the relevant actual acts or legal acts must have a sufficient substantive connection to the activities carried out in the performance of the statutory tasks of the AFM or DNB.

Sometimes, the AFM and DNB must take into account conflicting interests when performing their tasks. This may mean that it is certain or foreseeable to the AFM or DNB that a certain act will induce losses for a certain group of stakeholders. For example, early intervention or application for WDCCI (the write-down or conversion of capital instruments) by DNB for a bank (see Nos 59 and 60) generally could lead to losses for depositors, employees and shareholders. The withdrawal of an investment firm's licence by the AFM may have similar consequences (see No 16). Awareness of such harmful consequences does not in itself amount to an intentional act or gross negligence that could lead to liability. For this qualification, the following is required:

'an act or omission as a result of which an improper and objectionable performance of tasks or exercise of powers to such extent that it can be stated that the damage is the result of an intentional improper performance of duties or an intentional improper exercise of powers, or that the damage is due to gross negligence.' (Parliamentary History II 2011/12, 33 058, No 3).

In the context of an intentional act, the AFM or DNB must deliberately aim to neglect their tasks, or, if this is not the intention, the regulators must be aware that a certain act or omission will result in the improper performance of their tasks or will, in all probability, result in the improper performance of their tasks (intent in the capacity as awareness of certainty or conditional intent).

19 Cooperation between regulators

Cooperation between the AFM and DNB

The FSA prescribes mandatory cooperation between the AFM and DNB on several subjects (Section 1.3.1). The purpose of the cooperation provisions is to maximise the benefits of the functional supervision model.

The cooperation between the AFM and DNB relates to the following:

- determining general binding regulation, and policy rules (Art. 1:46 FSA);
- asking for the opinion of the other regulator before a decision to exercise a far-reaching measure is made such as the appointment of a silent trustee or the withdrawal of a licence (Art. 1:47 FSA);
- consultation by the AFM of DNB or the ECB before a licence is granted to certain investment firms (Art. 1:47a FSA);
- possibility for the AFM to advise before DNB grants a declaration of no objection to certain parties (Art. 1:47b FSA);
- requesting advice and informing the other regulator in the context of assessing the suitability of a director or supervisory director of a financial firm (Art. 1:47c FSA); and
- requesting advice from the AFM in the context of handling a licence
- application by DNB in respect of compliance with Part 3, and vice versa in respect of compliance with Part 4 (Art. 1:48 FSA).

Cooperation with other supervisors/European institutions

The international cooperation can be distinguished in cooperation with:

- regulators of other member states;

- regulators of non-member states; and
- European institutions, such as the European Commission and the ECB.

For example, this cooperation relates to:
- exchange of data and information;
- monitoring compliance with the FSA;
- enforcement;
- consultation and notification with respect to certain procedures and decisions; and
- provision of information in relation to reinsurers, life insurers or non-life insurers that are seated in a non-member state.

Both the AFM and DNB have concluded certain agreements with various bodies in member states (and non-member states as well) in so-called Memoranda of Understanding.

20 Procedures; licence and DNO

Licence

If Part 2 stipulates that a licence is required for a certain activity, it must be obtained from the AFM or DNB. Chapter 1.6 lays down rules concerning the procedure for obtaining that licence. For each licence, the MAFUD lays down more detailed rules on the application, and the documents and information that must be submitted.

The licence is applied by means of a form that is available on the website of the AFM or DNB. The AFM or DNB must decide within 13 weeks after receipt of the licence application (Art. 1:102 FSA). A few exemptions may apply to this term:

- in relation to a UCITS or a depositary a term of eight weeks applies (Art. 1:102 (4) FSA); and
- in relation to an AIFM a term of 26 weeks applies, but if the regulator anticipates that it needs more than thirteen weeks, it will inform the applicant accordingly (Art. 1:102(5) FSA).

If the AFM or DNB requests additional information, the term is paused and starts running again once the information has been provided by the applicant.

All licence holders can be found in the register maintained by the AFM or DNB (Art. 1:107 FSA).

Amendment and/or withdrawal

Under certain circumstances, the regulator may amend, withdraw or restrict, in whole or in part, a licence that has been granted, or attach further requirements to the licence, including under the following circumstances:

- on the basis of a request by the licence holder;
- in the event of incorrect provision of information at the time of the licence application;
- if the licence has not been used within twelve months of granting; and
- in the event of changed circumstances as a result of which the licence holder no longer complies with the applicable licence requirements (Art. 1:104(1) FSA).

Additionally, the licence is withdrawn in specific cases:

- an insurer does not meet the minimum capital requirements and DNB considers its short-term financial plan as insufficient (see No 45);

- an insurer does not carry out the short-term financial plan within three months; and
- the regulator agrees to a portfolio transfer (Art. 1:104(2) FSA).

Declaration of no objection

Specific procedural provisions govern the application to acquire or increase a qualifying holding, which deviate from those governing the application for a licence, which apply mutatis mutandis. (Arts. 1:105 FSA, 1:106a FSA-1:106e FSA). See No 50.

21 Remuneration policy

As a result of the financial crisis, a lot of attention was given to remuneration in the financial sector on both a national and international level, particularly because of the possible perverse incentives of variable remuneration (bonuses).

At a European level, the remuneration rules for banks and investment firms are laid down in CRD. These rules only apply to so-called 'Identified Staff'. These are employees whose activities have a material impact on the risk profile of the financial firm (including the management board).

The Dutch legislator has gone a step further and included stricter rules in Section 1.7. These rules relate to:
- balanced remuneration policy;
- disclosure requirements;
- maximum variable pay ('20% bonus cap');
- prohibition on guaranteed variable pay;
- maximum severance pay;

- clawback and adjustment of variable pay; and
- prohibition on variable pay in the event of state aid.

20% bonus cap

The most discussed rule is requirement on the maximum variable pay of 20%. A financial firm may not grant variable pay higher than 20% of the fixed annual remuneration to its employees (Art. 1:121 FSA). Variable pay is any pay that is not fixed.

Scope

These remuneration rules apply to:

- all financial firms having their seat in the Netherlands. Additionally, the remuneration rules listed above apply to the entire group (within the meaning of Art. 2:24b DCC) if the main activities of the group consist of offering financial products or providing financial services. The bonus cap also applies to Dutch branches of financial firms having their seat in another member state; and
- all natural persons working under responsibility of the relevant financial firm and not just to 'Identified Staff'.

Exemptions

Exemptions to this bonus cap may be available for:

- employees that are part of a group of persons of which the variable pay is not exclusively subject to a collective labour agreement. This exemption only applies if the average relationship between fixed and variable pay across the group of such individuals (not being subject to a collective labour agreement) does not exceed 20%;
- persons working mainly in another member state (at least 50% of the hours worked): they are subject to a bonus cap of 100%;

- persons working mainly in a non-member state: they are subject to a bonus cap of 200%;
- a group with an international character: a bonus cap of 100% applies if 75% of all natural persons worked outside of the Netherlands for at least three years over the last five years; and
- AIFMs, UCITS management companies, and investment firms that exclusively deal on their own account.

Claw-back and adjustment of bonuses

The amount of the variable pay must be adjusted to an appropriate level if the bonus 'is considered to be unacceptable according to standards of reasonableness and fairness' (Art. 1:126 FSA in conjunction with Art. 2:135(6) DCC). In addition, variable pay is subject to a claw-back if the payment was made on the basis of incorrect information on the achievement of the targets underlying the payment of the variable pay or on the circumstances on which the bonus depends (Art. 1:126 FSA; Art. 2:135(8) DCC).

III Market Access Financial Firms (Part 2)

22 *Introduction*

Basically, Part 2 consists of two sections:

- The first section contains all licence obligations and the related licensing requirements for financial firms that intend to operate on the Dutch financial markets (Chapter 2.2).
- The second section contains the rules for financial firms that are licensed on the basis of Chapter 2.2 and intend to operate in foreign financial markets (Chapter 2.3).

Prohibition, unless

The licence obligations for the various activities are formulated as prohibitions. This means that, in principle, an activity is prohibited unless a licence has been obtained from the competent regulator. In certain cases, it is not necessary to obtain a licence (see No 24).

It should be noted that not all prohibitions are listed in Part 2. See for example:

- Arts. 3:5 FSA, 3:6 FSA, 3:7 FSA, 3:95 FSA, 4:3 FSA, 5:25k FSA, 5:25l FSA, 5:26 FSA, 5:32d FSA, 5:74 FSA (applicable to any person);
- Arts. 3:35 FSA, 3:36 FSA, 3:38 FSA, 3:38a FSA, 3:51 FSA, 3:62b FSA; and 3:96 FSA, 3:97 FSA, 4:60 FSA and 4:74 FSA (applicable to certain licensed financial firms).

Licensed activities

The following activities trigger a licence obligation:

- conducting the business of a
  - settlement institution (Art. 2:3.0b FSA);
  - payment service provider (Art. 2:3a FSA);
  - depositary (Art. 2:3g FSA);
  - clearing institution (Art. 2:4 FSA);
  - electronic money institution (Art. 2:10a FSA);
  - bank (Art. 2:11 FSA);
  - financial institution (Arts. 2:24 FSA and 3:110 FSA);
  - reinsurer (Art. 2:26a FSA);
  - life insurer or non-life insurer (Art. 2:27 FSA);
  - life insurer, funeral expenses and benefits in-kind insurer or small non-life insurer with limited risks (Art. 2:48 FSA);
  - entity for risk acceptance (Art. 2:54a FSA);
  - premium pension institution (**PPI**) (Art. 2:54g FSA);
  - exchange institution (Art. 2:54i FSA); or
  - credit union (Art. 2:54o FSA).
- offering investment objects (Art. 2:55 FSA);
- offering credit (Art. 2:60 FSA);
- managing and marketing units in alternative investment funds and UCITS (Arts. 2:65 FSA and 2:69b FSA);
- advising on financial products other than financial instruments (Art. 2:75 FSA);
- acting as an intermediary (Art. 2:80 FSA);
- acting as a reinsurance intermediary (Art. 2:86 FSA);
- acting as an authorised agent or subauthorised agent (Art. 2:92 FSA);
- providing investment services and performing investment activities (Art. 2:96 FSA); or
- providing data reporting services (Art. 2:103c FSA).

In this chapter we will discuss some of these activities in further detail.

Licensing authority

DNB is the licensing authority for the activities listed up to Art. 2:54o FSA (excluding Art. 2:3g FSA) and the AFM is the licensing authority for the activities listed from Art. 2:55 FSA up to Art. 2:103c FSA. Consequently, there is only one regulator authorised to grant a licence for each type of licensable activity. In certain cases, the licensing authority has to assess elements during the licensing process that do not belong to its domain. In such cases, it is necessary that the non-licensing authority is also able to contribute its expertise to the licensing process and is substantively involved in the assessment prior to market entry (Art. 1:48 FSA).

For example:
For banks that also intend to provide investment services or perform investment activities, DNB will seek advice from the AFM on the elements of market conduct that are relevant to investment services or investment activities (Art. 2:13 FSA).

Single Supervisory Mechanism and ECB competence

On the basis of the Single Supervisory Mechanism (**SSM**), the ECB carries out prudential supervision of 'significant' Dutch banks. The ECB is also the licensing authority for banks.

Art. 17d of the PRD gives substance to the concept of significant relevance in relation to banks. The main rule is that DNB assesses whether a bank is of significant relevance (second paragraph). In any case, banks subject to ECB supervision under the SSM Regulation (Regulation (EU) No 1024/2013) are considered to be of significant relevance.

A bank is subject to the ECB's supervision if it is deemed to be an institution of significant relevance within the meaning of Art. 6 of that Regulation. This is the case if it meets certain quantitative criteria or if the ECB, on its own initiative, has considered it to be an institution of significant relevance, and in any case if it belongs to the three most important national banks.

If a bank (or its financial holding company) established at the highest consolidated level within the consolidated group meets one of the following criteria, it qualifies as significant (see Art. 6(4) SSM Regulation and Art. 53(1) SSM Framework Regulation (Regulation (EU) No 468/2014)):

- the total value of assets exceeds €30 billion;
- the ratio of its total assets to the gross national product of the member state of establishment exceeds 20%;
- the institution has received support from the *European Financial Stability Facility* or the *European Stability Mechanism*; or
- the institution is one of the three most significant banks in the relevant member state.

In the Netherlands, the following banks have been identified as significant:

- ABN AMRO;
- ING Bank;
- Rabobank;
- Volksbank;
- Bank Nederlandse Gemeenten; and
- Nederlandse Waterschapsbank.

23 *Territorial scope*

In the Netherlands

Certain prohibitory provisions in Part 2 only relate to financial services or the offering of financial products 'in the Netherlands' (see *e.g.* Arts. 2:60 and 2:96 FSA). This means that the relevant activities must be aimed at Dutch residents.

- *'The element "from the Netherlands" is not integrated into the FSA (from the FSPA (old)), because the granting of licenses to companies established in the Netherlands that exclusively provide services to foreign clients does not fit in with the objective of this proposal which is to regulate the provision of financial services on the Dutch financial markets by means of a licence obligation.'* (Parliamentary History II 2005/06, 29 708, No 19)
- *If investment services are provided by foreign undertakings to Dutch clients, exclusively on the initiative of those clients, the provision of such services is not deemed to take place in the Netherlands. This is being referred to as the 'initiative test' or 'reverse enquiry'* (Art. 1:19c(a) FSA).

Services via Internet

An exemption applies to services provided via the internet in another member state by financial firms established in the Netherlands. Such services do fall within the scope of the FSA (see No 14).

To act as insurance intermediary for clients located outside the Netherlands

Another exemption may be available for undertakings advising on insurances, acting as intermediary in insurances and reinsurances from the Netherlands for clients in another member state (Art. 1:22 FSA). Such services are also considered to take place 'in the Netherlands'.

Seat in the Netherlands

Other prohibitory provisions in Part 2 apply only to financial services provided by financial firms 'having their seat (zetel) in the Netherlands' (see *e.g.* Arts. 2:11 and 2:27 FSA). In such cases there are no restrictions to the territorial scope of the prohibitions and it then becomes irrelevant where and to whom the services are provided.

'There is reason to exercise prudential supervision over financial firms that carry out activities "from" the Netherlands. Prudential supervision is aimed at protecting the soundness of financial firms and at contributing to the stability of the financial sector. Such solidity and stability may also be affected by activities that are conducted abroad. (...) For that reason, the prudential supervision on a financial firm having its seat in the Netherlands must extend to the activities it conducts in another Member State'. (Parliamentary History II 2004/05, 29 708, No 10)

24 Statutory exemptions and dispensations

A licence is not required if:

- the activity is out of scope;
- a statutory exemption applies;
- a licence is 'passported' from another member state by means of a notification (see No 25);
- a (ministerial) derogation applies; or
- a dispensation has been obtained from the competent supervisor.

For example:
In relation to the licence obligation for the provision of investment services (Art. 2:96 FSA) the following may apply:

- *Scoping provision in Art. 1:18 FSA;*

- *Statutory exemptions in Art. 2:97 FSA;*
- *The possibility of passporting in Art. 2:98 FSA;*
- *Exemption in Art. 2:104 FSA and Arts. 10-14 FSA Exemption Regulation; and*
- *The possibility of a dispensation granted by the supervisor in Art. 2:96 FSA.*

Scope of application

Exemptions to the licence obligations are set out in Part 1 in the form of scope clauses (see No 14).

Statutory exemptions

Exemptions to the licence obligations are also set out in Part 2, stipulated directly below the relevant prohibitory provisions. This includes for example:

- other regulated financial firms that do not require an additional licence for a certain activity (see *e.g.* Art. 2:61 FSA that allows licensed banks and insurers to offer credit); and
- small/'light' AIFMs, for which we refer to No 32 (Art. 2:66a FSA).

Exemption Regulation

Exemptions from the licence obligations can also be found in the FSA Exemption Regulation. See:

- Art. 2:3d FSA in conjunction with 1a FSA Exemption Regulation and Art. 1b FSA Exemption Regulation (payment institutions);
- Art. 2:3h FSA in conjunction with 1c FSA Exemption Regulation (depositaries);
- Art. 2:10d FSA in conjunction with 1d FSA Exemption Regulation (electronic money institutions);

- Art. 2:49b FSA in conjunction with 1e FSA Exemption Regulation and Art. 1f FSA Exemption Regulation (funeral expenses and benefits in-kind insurers and non-life insurers);
- Art. 2:54o FSA in conjunction with 1g FSA Exemption Regulation (funeral expenses and benefits-in kind insurers and non-life insurers);
- Art. 2:54q FSA in conjunction with 1j FSA Exemption Regulation (credit unions);
- Art. 2:59 FSA in conjunction with 2 FSA Exemption Regulation (offering of investment objects);
- Art. 2:64 FSA in conjunction with 3 FSA Exemption Regulation, 3a FSA Exemption Regulation, 3b FSA Exemption Regulation and 3c FSA Exemption Regulation (offering of credit);
- Art. 2:79 FSA in conjunction with 5 FSA Exemption Regulation and 5a FSA Exemption Regulation (advising);
- Art. 2:85 FSA in conjunction with 6 FSA Exemption Regulation, Art. 6a FSA Exemption Regulation and Art. 7 FSA Exemption Regulation (acting as an intermediary);
- Art. 2:91 FSA in conjunction with 8 FSA Exemption Regulation (acting as a reinsurance intermediary);
- Art. 2:95 FSA in conjunction with 9 FSA Exemption Regulation (acting as an authorised agent or an indirect authorised agent); and
- Art. 2:104 FSA in conjunction with 10-18 FSA Exemption Regulation (providing investment services and performing investment activities).

Although there is a statutory basis for an exemption for the following activity, the Dutch Minister of Finance has not (no longer) given further substance to such exemption:

- Art. 2:74 FSA (marketing of units in and managing of investment institutions).

Dispensations

Provisions that facilitate dispensation from the licence obligations are listed directly under the relevant prohibitory provisions in Part 2:

- Art. 2:54i(3) FSA (exchange institutions);
- Art. 2:55(2) FSA (offering of investment objects);
- Art. 2:60(2) FSA (offering of credit);
- Art. 2:75(2) FSA (advising);
- Art. 2:80(2) FSA (acting as an intermediary);
- Art. 2:86(2) FSA (acting as a reinsurance intermediary);
- Art. 2:92(2) FSA (acting as an authorised agent or subauthorised agent); and
- Art. 2:96(2) FSA (providing investment services and performing investment activities).

These 'serious' dispensations may be subject to certain restrictions and may be granted in part or for a limited period of time. In addition, the supervisor may subject these dispensations to certain regulations (Art. 1:10(1) under (c) FSA in conjunction with Art. 1:102(2) FSA). The withdrawal of the 'serious' dispensation decision can be done both on the supervisor's own initiative and upon request (Art. 1:10(1) under (c) FSA in conjunction with Art. 1:104 FSA).

By operation of law versus on request

If a party satisfies the conditions of an exemption, it is exempted from the licence obligation by operation of law. However, dispensation must be applied for and shall be granted by the relevant supervisor only to the extent that the applicant demonstrates that the interests intended to be protected by Parts 2, 3 and 4 (each to the extent applicable) are sufficiently protected by other means.

Relationship to ongoing supervisory requirements

If a licence is not required in connection with any of the above, this does not automatically mean that the relevant firm is also exempt from the ongoing supervision requirements in Parts 3 and 4.

- However, this may be the case with regard to certain scope provisions (see *e.g.* Art. 1:18 FSA).
- If statutory exemptions apply, an exemption to the ongoing supervision requirements in Part 3 and 4 does not apply, due to the compartmentalised design of the FSA (*e.g.* Art. 2:66a FSA in conjunction with 15 FSA Exemption Regulation with regard to Part 3).
- If exemptions under the FSA Exemption Regulation apply , this is not the case due to the compartmentalised design of the FSA. However, where this is intended by the legislator, this is provided for in the FSA Exemption Regulation (see *e.g.* Art. 14 FSA Exemption Regulation in conjunction with 18 FSA Exemption Regulation and 36 FSA Exemption Regulation with regard to Part 3 and Part 4 respectively).
- For European passport holders, the 'home country control' or 'home state supervision' principle generally applies with respect to ongoing supervision. Exemptions apply to:
  - liquidity supervision on banks (Art. 3:64 FSA); and
  - Part 4 rules for investment firms having their seat in another member state and having a Dutch branch (Art. 4:1(2) FSA).

25 European passport

Basically, the 'European passport' is a licence obtained in one member state which can be used for unimpeded access to other member states, as a result of which no separate licence needs to be obtained in such other member state (see *e.g.* Art. 2:98(2) under (a) and under (b) FSA). The European passport is only available to financial firms regulated on the basis of European legislation, such as MiFID (see No 4).

A financial firm based in another member state can use its European passport in the Netherlands in two ways:

- through a branch office in the Netherlands; and
- without a branch, by means of cross-border 'provision of services'.

However, a firm looking to rely on a European passport must first go through the notification procedure (see No 37).

26 Payment service providers

Description

A payment service provider is '*a person who provides payment services as a regular occupation or business activity*' (Art. 1:1 FSA). A 'payment service' is a '*business activity as referred to in the annex to the payment services directive*', being:

- services enabling cash to be placed on or withdrawn from a payment account and all operations required for operating such payment account;

- execution of various types of payment transactions with or without being covered by a credit line, including the execution of one-off direct debits or standing orders, the execution of payment transactions by means of a payment card or a similar device and credit transfers;
- issuing of payment instruments and/or acquiring of payment transactions;
- money remittance;
- payment initiation services; and
- account information services.

As soon as a payment service provider has obtained a licence, it is being referred to as a 'payment institution'.

Statutory exemption

The rules relating to the provision of information pursuant to Art. 4:22(2) FSA, which are further specified in Arts. 59b-59g of the MCSD, only apply if the payment services are offered in the Netherlands (Art. 1:5a (1) FSA).

A number of activities is excluded from the scope of the definition of 'payment services' (Art. 1:5a(2) FSA). Although these activities fall outside the scope of the prohibition of Art. 2:3a FSA, this does not necessarily mean that such activities are unregulated. For example, a money exchange transaction falls within scope of the licence obligation for exchange institutions (Art. 1:5a(2) under (f) FSA).

In addition, licensed banks and electronic money institutions are exempted from the licence obligation (Art. 2:3a (2) FSA).

Exemption Regulation

A payment service provider that provides certain payment services in the Netherlands and also meets the other requirements of Art. 1a(1) FSA Exemption Regulation is exempted from the licence obligation (Art. 1a FSA Exemption Regulation). In order to make use of the exemption, DNB must have been notified. However, such exempted payment service providers are subject to ongoing supervision requirements.

27 Electronic money institutions

Description

An 'electronic money institution' is '*the one conducting the business of the issuance of electronic money*'. Furthermore, '*electronic money*' is a '*monetary value which is stored electronically or magnetically and which represents a claim on the issuer, and which is issued in exchange for money in order to carry out payment transactions as referred to in Art. 4 under 5 of the payment services directive, and with which payments can be made to another person than the issuer*' (Art. 1:1 FSA). This definition covers all situations where a firm issues a pre-paid stored value in exchange for money, and where such value is accepted by third parties.

Statutory exemption

The following payment instruments are excluded from the rules that are applicable to electronic money:

- instruments that can only be used by the electronic money holder to purchase goods etc. from the electronic money issuer, from one particular store or from one particular chain of stores (*e.g.* a customer card of a particular retail chain); and

- instruments with a limited use, meaning that only a very limited range of goods or services can be purchased with the electronic money (*e.g.* fuel cards, cards for public transport, meal vouchers or service vouchers) (Art. 1:5 FSA).

In addition, licensed banks are exempted from the licence obligation (Art. 2:10a(2) FSA).

Exemption Regulation

An electronic money institution that complies with the requirements of Art. 1b(1) FSA Exemption Regulation is exempt from the licence obligation. In order to make use of such exemption, DNB must have been notified. Also in this case, the ongoing supervisory requirements for electronic money institutions remain applicable.

28 Banks

Description

For the definition of bank in Art. 1:1 FSA, reference is made to the definition of 'credit institution' within the meaning of Art. 4 Capital Requirements Regulation (Regulation (EU) No 575/2013, **CRR**). The definition of credit institution in Art. 4 CRR reads: '*an undertaking the business of which is to take deposits or other repayable funds from the public and to grant credits for its own account*'. The core elements of these provisions are undefined, but can be traced back to the interpretations of pre-CRR terminology.

- **'deposits or other repayable funds'**
  These are funds that, for whatever reason, must be repaid at some point, and of which it is clear in advance what nominal amount is to be repaid. For example, borrowing money or issuing a bond. Funds attracted by issuing shares do not qualify as repayable funds: in the case of shares, no obligation exists to repay the nominal amount. Furthermore, the following categories are not considered repayable funds:
  - paper vouchers and casino chips;
  - a prepayment for a specific purchase transaction;
  - a permitted deferral of payment for a specific sales transaction; and
  - funds that have been received in the context of a specific order for a 'payment transfer' to a third party (Art. 4 CRR).

If, in the case of a payment transfer, the period between giving the order to transfer the payment and receipt by the third party exceeds five calendar days, in principle, the funds are repayable.

- **Public**
  The funds should be attracted from the 'public' (see No 8).
- **Granting of credits**
  The granting of nominally repayable funds to another person with the aim of obtaining benefits. The benefits for the lender or a related party have to be 'assessable in money'.
- **For its own account**
  The lender itself is exposed to the financial risk attached to granting the credit. If the lender receives a profit or loss-related fee for lending, he or she also acts 'for its own account'. The same applies if the risk of a loan granted is covered by a guarantee or

an identical loan agreement ('back-to-back') with a third lender or investor.

- **The business of which is**
  This is being construed as 'conducting the business of'. This is the case if:
  - the banking business is an independently identifiable activity; and
  - the activity does not serve exclusively to support the main activities of the relevant firm.

If the main activities are of a financial nature, it is irrelevant whether attracting and lending of the funds is supporting the main activities. If the main activities are not of a financial nature, such as in the case of an undertaking that attracts funds for the benefit of its own business or the business of its (non-financial) operating companies, this qualifying factor does not apply.

Statutory exemption

An exemption to the licence obligation applies to group finance companies (see No 39).

29 Insurers

The term 'insurers' is a catch-all term for:

- life insurers;
- non-life insurers;
- funeral expenses and benefits-in kind insurers; and
- reinsurers.

Description

Non-life insurers

A non-life insurer is '*a person that conducts the business of arranging non-life insurance contracts for its own account and settles those non-life insurances*'. A non-life insurance is:

- a non-life insurance as referred to in Art. 7:944 DCC, not being a funeral expenses and benefits-in kind insurance;
- a casualty insurance; or
- an insurance providing for payment of a capital sum as referred to in Art. 7:964 DCC, not being a life insurance or a financial instrument.

Note that it follows from the above that an otc derivative, such as a 'credit default swap', does not qualify as an insurance under the FSA (since it qualifies as a financial instrument).

Life insurers

A life insurer is '*a person that conducts the business of arranging life insurance contracts for its own account and settles those life insurances*'. Life insurances are:

- insurances within the meaning of Art. 7:975 DCC, provided that the payment by the life insurer exclusively takes place in money; or
- funeral expenses and benefits in-kind insurance.

Funeral expenses and benefits in kind insurance

A funeral expenses and benefits in-kind insurer is '*a person, not being a life insurer, that conducts the business of arranging funeral expenses and benefits in-kind insurance contracts for his own account and settles such contracts*'. A funeral expenses and benefits in-kind insurance relates to arranging the funeral of a natural person, under which the insurer undertakes to provide a service that does not involve making a monetary payment.

Reinsurers

A reinsurer is '*a person that conducts the business of arranging reinsurance contracts for its own account and settles those reinsurance contracts*'. A reinsurance is an insurance whereby risks are accepted that are transferred from one insurer to another.

Statutory exemptions

Excluded from Part 2 and thus from the licence obligation are, amongst others (but not limited to):

- certain institutions representing certain public interests (*e.g.* the Social Insurance Bank (SVB), the Employee Insurance Agency (UWV) and certain health insurance funds) (Art. 1:6 FSA);
- certain reinsurers designated by the Minister as necessary for public interests (*e.g.* the Dutch Terrorism Risk Reinsurance Company (**NHT**) (Art. 1:6a FSA); and
- Pension funds that implement a pension plan (Art. 1:8 FSA).

In addition, licensed funeral expenses and benefits in-kind insurers are exempted from the licence obligation for life insurers to the extent they exclusively conduct the business of a funeral expenses and benefits in-kind insurer (Art. 2:27(3) FSA). The same (reversed) exemption applies to licensed life insurers with regard to the licence obligation for funeral expenses and benefits in-kind insurers (Art. 2:48 (3) FSA).

Exemption Regulation

Funeral expenses and benefits in-kind insurers and non-life insurers with limited risks are exempt from the licence obligation (Art. 2:49b FSA in conjunction with Art. 1e and 1f FSA Exemption Regulation).

Miscellaneous

Insurers (not being reinsurers) may also conduct the business of reinsurer for their insurance business without an additional licence (Art. 2:26a(3) FSA).

A licensed insurer may conduct either the business of life insurer or the business of non-life insurer but not both ('combination ban', Art. 2:28 FSA).

In addition, it is prohibited to conduct a business other than the insurance business for which the insurer has been granted a licence ('prohibition of ancillary business', Art. 3:36 FSA).

Life insurers, funeral expenses and benefits in-kind insurers, and non-life insurers with limited risks are subject to a national regime with less stringent licence obligation (resulting from the implementation of the Solvency II Directive). Insurers eligible for such national regime must apply for a licence from DNB (Art. 2:48 FSA)

30 *Offering investment objects*

Description

An investment object is:

- an item of property, a right to an item of property or a right to the full or partial return in money or part of the proceeds of (the sale of) an item of property;
- that is acquired other than for no consideration (*e.g.* for payment in kind);
- with the prospect of a return in cash (*i.e.* a return in kind does not qualify as such); and
- for which the management is mainly carried out by someone else than the acquirer (Art. 1:1 FSA).

An investment object is an individual investment that is identifiable as such, since it must qualify as an item of property or a right derived from such item. Consequently, an investment object therefore does not comprise a unit in a collective investment scheme (however, such unit could qualify as a unit in an AIF).

On its website, the AFM has identified a number of objects that qualify as investment objects, such as lots of agricultural land, recreational real estate, teak participations and ostrich eggs. Additionally, the FSA Definitions Decree defines certain rights as investment objects, such as participation rights in film-limited partnerships.

Solely the offering of investment objects to consumers is subject to a licence obligation. This follows from the definition of 'offering' in Art. 1:1 FSA. Please refer to Nos 8 and 13 for the definitions of 'consumers' and 'offering'.

Statutory exemptions

Licensed banks and insurers are excluded from the licence obligation (Art. 2:56 FSA).

Exemption Regulation

An exemption from the licence obligation is available if the relevant investment objects:

- are offered to less than 100 consumers;
- are part of a series consisting of less than twenty investment objects (a series consists of investment objects with the same characteristics);
- have a value that cannot be determined; or
- are offered for at least € 100,000 per unit (Art. 2 FSA Exemption Regulation).

In the above cases, the offeror is also exempted from market conduct supervision in Part 4 (Art. 43 FSA Exemption Regulation). However, if an exemption is applicable a warning prescribed by the AFM (the 'wild west sign') must be included in the offeror's advertisements (see No 79).

31 *Offering credit*

Description

The definition of 'credit' in Art. 1:1 FSA stipulates that there are two types of credit: money credit and credit for goods:

- Money credit refers to the extension of credit to a consumer as a result of which the consumer is provided with direct access to a sum of money in respect of which one or more payments must be made (*e.g.* a (mortgage) loan).
- Credit for goods refers to the extension of credit to a consumer as a result of which the consumer must make one or more payments. Such purchasing financing may relate to the following:

- the provision of a service;
- allowing the use of a movable property, financial instrument or investment object; or
- the provision of direct access to a sum of money to a consumer or a third party in respect of the future provision of a service or the use of a movable property, financial instrument or investment object (*e.g.* a car that is purchased in instalments).

On 13 June 2014 (JOR 2014/206), the Supreme Court ruled that offering a telephone subscription in combination with a 'free' telephone is regarded as 'offering credit'.

Only the offering of credit to *consumers* is subject to a licence obligation. This follows from the definition of 'offering' in Art. 1:1 FSA. This is why the term 'consumer credit' is often used in everyday speech. For the terms 'consumers' and 'offering', see Nos 8 and 13.

Statutory exemptions

An exemption to the licensing obligation for the offering credit applies to credit that must be repaid within three months and for which insignificant costs are charged (Art. 1:20 FSA). In any case, such credit includes purchases on account and purchases in instalments (provided that the costs charged are insignificant and repayment must take place within three months). The costs referred to are considered to include interest as well as any other types of costs. The costs are considered to be insignificant in relative terms when they amount to only a very small percentage of the credit. However, the costs can also be insignificant in absolute terms. Furthermore, 'payday loans', for which interest and costs are charged, do not fall under the exemption.

In addition, licensed banks and insurers are exempt from the licensing requirement for the offering of credit (Art. 2:61(1) FSA).

Exemption Regulation

Exemptions apply to:

- securitisation SPVs, to the extent that the administration and the execution of the credit agreements is carried out by a licensed credit manager (Art. 3 FSA Exemption Regulation);
- certain bridge loans to natural persons by certain ecclesiastical, ideological, charitable, cultural, scientific or public institutions (*e.g.* the Salvation Army) at low interest or costs, to the extent such bridge loans are provided with clear and complete information on duties and obligations (Art. 3a FSA Exemption Regulation);
- licensed payment service providers, to the extent they offer credit in connection with the payment services referred to in points 4 and 5 of the Annex to the payment services directive provided that the funds received (in accordance with Art. 40c PRD) are secured (Art. 3b FSA Exemption Regulation); and
- persons who grant postponement of payment free of charge in relation to a claim that arises from certain credit agreement (Art. 3c FSA Exemption Regulation).

32 *Managing and offering of units in AIFs and UCITS*

The prohibitory provision regarding AIFs is less straightforward. In short, the following activities are subject to a licence obligation:

- the management of a Dutch AIF;
- the offering of units in an AIF in the Netherlands; or
- as a Dutch AIFM:

- the management of an AIF; or
- the offering of units in an AIF (Art. 2:65 FSA).

Offering a unit in a UCITS in the Netherlands is also an activity subject to a licence obligation (Art. 2:69b FSA).

The prohibitions do not apply if the AIFM or (in the case it concerns an investment company that does not have a separate manager) the investment company is licensed by the AFM.

An AIF or a UCITS structured as an investment company must have a separate manager, unless the company has equity of more than €300,000 (Arts. 4:37c and 4:58 FSA).

Taking into consideration great similarity between the rules applicable to AIFs and UCITS, we will only discuss the rules applicable to AIFs below.

Description

The 'management of an AIF' (Art. 1:1 FSA) entails the performance of the following two core tasks:

- **portfolio management**: determining the investment policy and making investment decisions;
- **risk management**: identifying, analysing and mitigating risks arising from portfolio management.

Please refer to No 10 for the terms 'offering', 'investment fund', 'AIF', 'investment company' and 'UCITS'.

Statutory exemptions

Light managers

There is an exemption to the licence obligation for so-called 'light' managers, of which the total value of assets managed does not exceed the following thresholds:

- €100 million (including leveraged financing); or
- €500 million (excluding leverage financing), provided that no redemption rights are exercisable during a period of five years after the initial investment in the relevant AIF.

Managers that do not exceed these thresholds do not require a licence if they offer units:

- to professional investors;
- to less than 150 persons;
- if the units can only be acquired for a consideration of at least € 100,000; or
- if the nominal value per unit is at least € 100,000 (Art. 2:66a FSA).

However, such managers are required to:

- notify the AFM of the applicability of the light regime to themselves and the relevant AIFs they manage after which both the manager and the relevant AIFs are included in a public register;
- report periodically to DNB on the main financial instruments in which they trade and, their risk exposures and risk concentrations to the managed AIFs (Art. 2:66a (3) FSA); and
- unless they only offer units to professional investors, include a 'wild west sign' in their marketing material. This is a warning prescribed by the AFM that indicates that the manager is not subject to supervision (Art. 2:66a (6) FSA).

Figure 1 The 'wild west sign"

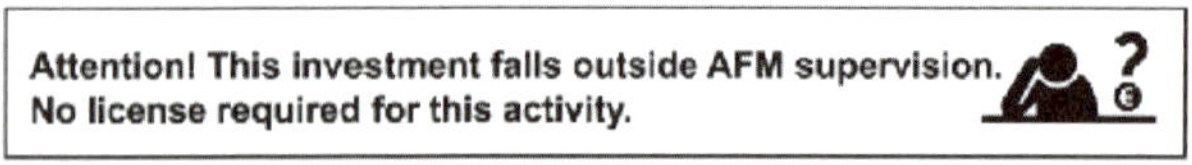

A similar sign exists for the exemptions from the prospectus obligation (see No 79).

Since these managers are exempted from the licence obligation, they are not subject to the ongoing supervision requirements set out in Part 4 (Art. 2:66a (6) FSA).

Excluded entities

The definition of AIF (see No 10) is quite broad. Therefore, a number of specific entities are exempted explicitly from the rules for AIFMs in the FSA:

- pension funds;
- holdings;
- supranational organisations and similar international organisations that manage AIFs to the extent such AIFs act in the public interest (*e.g.* the ECB, the European Investment Bank (EIB), the European Investment Fund (EIF), European Development Finance Institutions, bilateral development banks and the World Bank);
- national, regional and local governments and bodies of member states or other institutions that manage funds supporting social security and pension systems;
- Securitisation special purpose entities; and
- managers of AIFs in which investments are made exclusively by the managers themselves and their group companies, provided

that these managers and group companies do not qualify as AIFs (Art. 1:13a FSA).

Managers from non-EU countries

A statutory exemption is available for managers from a non-EU country (also referred to as a 'third country') that manage a Dutch AIF or offer units in AIFs to qualified/professional investors in the Netherlands (Art. 1:13b FSA). Such exemption is subject to the following conditions:

- the country in which the manager has its seat is not included on the *Financial Action Task Force*'s list of Non-Cooperative Countries and Territories; and
- the AFM and the regulator of the jurisdiction in which the manager is established have entered into a cooperation agreement that guarantees an efficient exchange of information.

Consequently, the manager is then exempt from the FSA. However, it must meet a number of specific requirements (see Art. 1:13b (2) FSA).

Managers from a designated state

Managers from a designated state are also exempt from the licence obligation (Art. 2:66 FSA). The Dutch Minister of Finance has designated Guernsey, Hong Kong SAR (in respect of the supervision of AIFs of which the units are offered to retail investors and which are registered with the *Securities and Futures Commission*), Jersey and the United States (only in respect of AIFs registered with the *Securities and Exchange Commission* (**SEC**)) as states of which the supervision is considered similar to Dutch supervision. This is the basis for the exemption from the licence obligation. If a manager from a designated state intends to offer units in the Netherlands, it must notify the AFM of this (Art. 2:73 FSA). Such notification must be accompanied by a certificate of its supervised statues by the supervisory authority in the state of origin.

The relationship between the regime for third country managers in Art. 1:13b FSA and managers from a designated state in Art. 2:66 FSA is as follows. Art. 2:66 FSA also covers the offering to non-professional investors whilst Art. 1:13b FSA exclusively covers the offering to professional investors. Therefore, the designated state regime does not apply to managers that are not allowed to offer to retail investors in their home state.

For example:
If a manager from the United States (of which the AIFS are SEC-registered) intends to offer units to professional investors in the Netherlands, it can rely on Art. 1:13b FSA. Consequently, it falls outside the scope of the FSA (with the exception of the articles referred to in Art. 1:13b(2) FSA). If such manager also intends to offer units to retail investors in the Netherlands, it can make use of Art. 2:66 FSA. This is only an exemption from the licence obligation (given the location of the exemption provision in the structure of the FSA). Therefore, for each element it must be examined whether the FSA applies.

Miscellaneous

The rules in the FSA relating to AIFs are addressed to their managers (Art. 1:13 FSA). If an investment company does not have a separate manager, the rules apply directly to such investment company.

Permitted 'extra' activities

De AFM may allow managers to provide certain investment services and ancillary services in addition to the management of AIFs (Art. 2:67a(2) FSA), specifically:

- the reception and transmission of orders (an investment service);
- the provision of individual portfolio management (an investment service);
- the provision of investment advice (an investment service); and
- the custody and administration of units in AIFs and UCITS (an ancillary service).

If the manager requests the AFM to also be permitted to provide these so-called '*top-up*' services, no separate licence is required for the provision of these investment services (Art. 2:97(3) FSA). However, the manager must comply with (additional) requirements from Part 4 that apply to investment firms.

Additionally, a manager with a licence to manage an AIF may also manage a UCITS, provided that it also has the required licence to do so (Art. 2:67a FSA in conjunction with Art. 2:69b FSA).

33 *Advising on financial products other than financial instruments*

Description

Advising is defined as the provision of recommendations in the pursuit of a profession or business to a specific consumer (or client, in respect of insurances and premium pension claims) in respect of one or more specific financial products other than financial instruments (Art. 1:1 FSA). Advising on financial instruments is therefore explicitly excluded. This requires a licence as an investment firm (see No 35).

It is important to note that the recommendation must relate to a specific financial product. Recommending a product type, *e.g.* a type of mortgage, does not qualify as advice. In addition, in order to qualify as advice, such advice should be tailored to the characteristics of a specific consumer (or client) and not to those of a general group (*e.g.* general advice included in marketing material).

Statutory exemptions

An exemption to the licence obligation and the ongoing supervision requirements in Part 4 applies to pension funds that provide financial services (including advising) to a business sector, company or profession to which they are affiliated (Art. 1:15 under a FSA).

Additionally, the following financial firms are exempt from the licence obligation:

- licensed banks, insurers and PPIs;
- financial firms licensed by the AFM for the provision of financial services other than advising, to the extent it concerns advice on a specific financial product (*e.g.* a financial firm that is licensed to act as a credit intermediary may also advise on credit);
- 'tied intermediaries', to the extent it concerns advising on the financial products for which they act as tied intermediaries; and
- intermediaries with a dispensation from the licence obligation for intermediaries, to the extent it concerns advising on the concerning financial product (Art. 2:76 FSA).

Exemption Regulation

Advisers who advise exclusively on certain types of financial products or to certain clients are exempt from the licensing requirement (Art. 5 and 5a FSA Exemption Regulation) or, depending on the products, from Part 4 (Art. 45 FSA Exemption Regulation).

34 *Acting as an intermediary*

Description

'Acting as an intermediary' means the performance, in the pursuit of a profession or business of all activities aimed at,

- by acting as an intermediary, the conclusion of:
  - an agreement regarding a financial product other than a financial instrument, credit, premium pension claim or an insurance between a consumer and an offeror;
  - a credit agreement between a consumer and an offeror or to assist in the administration and execution of such agreement;
  - an agreement which creates a premium pension claim between a PPI and a client or the assistance in the administration and execution of such agreement; and
  - an insurance agreement between a client and an insurer or the assistance in the management and execution of such insurance agreement; or
- providing information to a client about one or more financial products, which information is based on criteria selected by the client on a website or via other media (such as price or product comparisons), except financial instruments or the ranking of the relevant financial product (Art. 1:1 FSA).

The most important distinction is that in relation to acting as an intermediary in relation to credit, premium pension claims and insurance, the assistance in the administration and execution of the contract or insurance policy is also regarded as acting as an intermediary.

For example:
The collection of premiums on behalf of the insurer.

The term 'intermediary' (*tussenpersoon*) clarifies that the intermediary himself does not become a party to the relevant agreement.

Different legal proceedings were conducted on the scope of the definition of 'acting as an intermediary'. Solely forwarding the name, address and place of residence data does not amount to acting as an intermediary. As soon as other relevant data is added, such as annual income and information relating to registration with the Credit Registration Office, the outcome is different (see also Trade and Industry Appeals Tribunal (CBb) 11 February 2013, JOR 2013/112 and the AFM's publication on acting as an intermediary of September 2014).

Statutory exemption

A statutory exemption applies to licensed banks, PPIs and insurers (Art. 2:81 FSA).

Additionally, a statutory exemption applies to so-called 'tied intermediaries, that:

- act as an intermediary exclusively for one provider or, as long as the intermediation does regard competitive financial products, multiple providers; or
- in case of acting as an insurance intermediary, act on behalf and for the account of the insurer without collecting premiums, provided that the provider/insurer:
  - is fully responsible for the intermediary's actions; and
  - the relevant intermediary is registered with the AFM as a tied intermediary.

Exemption Regulation

Intermediaries that exclusively advise on certain types of financial products, or only advise in the context of other financial services, are exempt (Arts. 6 FSA Exemption Regulation and 7 FSA Exemption Regulation).

European passport

A European passport is only available for intermediaries in insurances or mortgages.

35 *Providing investment services and performing investment activities*

Description

The activities of an 'investment firm' are defined as the 'provision of investment services' and 'performance of investment activities' (see No 10)

Statutory exemptions

Exemptions apply to:

- intra-group operations;
- the administration of employee-participation plans;
- insurers;
- the provision of investment services only in an incidental manner in the context of a (other) professional activity (*e.g.* real estate brokers – to the extent that they are affiliated to a trade association that applies a professional code – that provide services on an incidental basis, for instance portfolio management);
- investment advice for which the providers are not specifically remunerated in the context of the provision of another

professional activity (*e.g.* real estate brokers and accountants who – not necessarily in an incidental manner – provide investment advice, but do not directly or indirectly get paid for such activity);

- operators subject to the directive establishing a system for greenhouse gas emission allowance trading, that do not execute client orders and exclusively trade on own account in relation to emission allowances, unless they apply high-frequency algorithmic trading;
- traders dealing on own account in financial instruments other than commodity derivatives or emission allowances (derivatives), unless such traders:
  - are market-makers;
  - are members or participants of a regulated market or MTF;
  - apply a high-frequency algorithmic trading technique; or
  - deal on own account when executing client orders; and
- traders dealing on own account in commodity derivatives or emission allowances (derivatives), if:
  - the dealing on own account or the provision of the investment service qualifies as an ancillary activity to the main business of the relevant trader;
  - the main business (of the group) does not consist of the provision of provision of investment services, banking activities or acting as a market-maker in relation to commodity derivatives;
  - no high-frequency algorithmic trading technique is applied; and
  - annual use of this exemption is notified to the AFM (Art. 1:18 FSA).

In addition, a statutory exemption applies in relation to investment services a and b regarding the purchase or sale of units in AIFs or UCITS by the managers of those AIFs or UCITS (Art. 1:19 FSA).

Finally, statutory exemptions from the licence obligation apply to:

- licensed banks to the extent that they are permitted to provide investment services or perform investment activities under their licence (see Art. 2:13 FSA);
- licensed managers of UCITS having their seat in the Netherlands, to the extent the relevant investment services concern individual portfolio management and the provision of advice on financial instruments;
- licensed managers of AIFs, to the extent the relevant investment services concern:
  - the provision of investment advice;
  - the provision of individual portfolio management; or
  - the reception and transmission of client orders in relation to financial instruments, in the pursuit of a profession or business; and
  - tied agents (if certain conditions are met) (Art. 2:97 FSA).

Exemption Regulation

Investment firms having their seat in Australia, the United States or Switzerland are exempt from the licence obligation if they are supervised for the provision of investment services in their home country (Art. 10 FSA Exemption Regulation). However, these firms must register with the AFM. They are also exempt from certain conduct of business rules of Part 4 (Art. 35 FSA Exemption Regulation). Additionally, they do not have to comply with prudential requirements (see No 9) (Art. 18 FSA Exemption Regulation).

In a *no-deal* Brexit scenario, investment firms seated in the United Kingdom, that provide investment services to professional investors in the Netherlands or deal for their own account, are temporarily exempt from the licence obligation in the Netherlands by a temporary extension of Art. 10 FSA Exemption Regulation. This exemption will only take effect in the case of a *no-deal* Brexit and is expected to end the earlier of 31 December 2020 and two years after it takes effect.

Ancillary services

In addition to the provision of investment services and the performance of investment activities, investment firms may also provide ancillary services. No independent licence obligation applies to the provision of these services. A licensed investment firm intending to provide ancillary services must notify the AFM of this intention (Art. 2:99(5) FSA). The background to this is that providing ancillary services is subject to certain conduct of business rules (see *e.g.* Art. 4:90 FSA). An 'ancillary service' means:

- the safekeeping and administration of financial instruments;
- the granting of credit to allow an investor to enter into transactions in financial instruments where the investment firm granting the credit is involved in the transaction;
- advising undertakings on capital structure, industrial strategy and related matters and advice and services relating to mergers and acquisitions;
- foreign exchange services where these are connected to the provision of investment services;
- investment research and financial analysis;
- investment services related to underwriting; and
- investment services or activities (and ancillary services) related to the underlying of the derivatives, to the extent that these are

related to the provision of investment or ancillary services (Art. 1:1 FSA).

36 Licence requirements

The licence requirements or ongoing supervision requirements for all financial firms can be distinguished into prudential and conduct of business requirements. For brevity's sake, these are referred to by reference to their location in Part 3 and Part 4 in the provisions, listing these requirements per licensed activity (see *e.g.* Art. 2:99 FSA for investment firms).

The licence requirements for financial firms that are required to obtain a licence from DNB (with the exception of clearing and settlement institutions and PPIs) are mostly included Part 3. However, certain conduct of business requirements from Part 4 (*e.g.* Art. 4:20 FSA, see No 69) also apply to them.

For financial firms that need to obtain a licence from the AFM (with the exception of UCITS management companies, AIFMs and investment firms), the licence requirements only relate to the conduct of business requirements from Part 4.

Generally, the following licence requirements apply to (almost) every licence application:

- suitability and trustworthiness of (daily) policy makers;
- integrity policy of the applicant;
- requirements regarding the minimum number of persons determining the day-to-day policy and the place from where such persons must carry out their activities;

- requirements relating to the structure of control of the applicant;
- requirements relating to the organisation of business operations;
- the minimum amount of own funds the applicant must retain; and
- the solvency of the applicant.

Depending on the activity or the type of financial firm, the licence application is subject to more or less stringent requirements. The rules in Part 3 and 4 will be explained in more detail in Nos 42-50 and Nos 64-77, where they will be discussed as rules for 'ongoing supervision'.

Light dispensations

In certain cases, it is possible to request for dispensation (partial or full) from one or more specific licence requirements:
- Art. 2:3.0d(4) FSA (settlement institutions);
- Art. 2:5(3) FSA (clearing institution);
- Art. 2:12(5) FSA (banks);
- Art. 2:26b(4) FSA (reinsurers);
- Art. 2:31(4) FSA (life and non-life insurers);
- Art. 2:49(3) FSA (funeral expenses and benefits-in kind insurers);
- Art. 2:54h(4) FSA (PPIs);
- Art. 2:54j(3) FSA (exchange institutions);
- Art. 2:54p(3) FSA (credit unions);
- Art. 2:58(3) FSA (offering of investment objects);
- Art. 2:63(3) FSA (offering of credit);
- Art. 2:67b(4) FSA (offering of units in and the management of AIFs);
- Art. 2:78(3) FSA (advising);
- Art. 2:83(3) FSA (acting as an intermediary);

- Art. 2:94(3) FSA (acting as authorised agent or subauthorised agent); and
- Art. 2:99 (6)FSA (provision of investment services, performance of investment activities).

Supervisors may not discretionarily make these 'light' dispensations subject to further rules. However, it is possible that the requirements to obtain a light dispensation are subject to rules laid down in in a ministerial decree (Art. 1:105(2) FSA). Light dispensations may be withdrawn (Art. 1:105(2) FSA).

In certain cases, a dispensation also applies to the ongoing supervision requirements in Part 3 and Part 4 (see Art. 2:2 FSA).

37 *Access to foreign financial markets; notification procedure*

Financial firms with a European passport (see No 25) have to complete a notification procedure before they can operate in another member state. This notification procedure is based on cooperation between supervisors in different member states. Below, we discuss the access of a Dutch financial firm to a foreign market (*e.g.* Germany). For foreign companies that intend to enter the Dutch market, this procedure is mirrored.

Establishing a branch

For the establishment of a branch in another member state, the following process applies:

- the financial firm must submit a request for consent to the 'home state regulator';

- the home state regulator agrees, unless the business operations and financial position of the financial firm are insufficient;
- the home state regulator reports its decision within three months to the regulator of the member state in which the branch is to be opened ('host state regulator');
- the host state regulator informs the home state regulator about any conditions it imposes in relation to conducting the relevant activities in its jurisdiction;
- within two months after such notification, the home state regulator reports to the financial firm to which conditions the host state regulator has subjected the conducting of the activities in that jurisdiction; and
- subsequently, the financial firm may open its branch in that member state (*e.g.* see Art. 2:127 FSA for the opening of a branch by a Dutch investment firm in another member state).

Without a branch – cross border

Where a financial firm intends to provide services in another member state without a branch, the process is as follows:

- a notification to the home state regulator suffices;
- directly after this notification, the financial firm may commence its activities in the host member state; and
- within one month, the home state regulator informs the host state regulator of the intention (see *e.g.* Art. 2:128 FSA).

IV Prudential Supervision of Financial Firms (Part 3)

38 *Introduction*

Scope

Part 3 contains the prudential rules applicable to financial firms. The majority of the rules in Part 3, including those on suitability, trustworthiness, integrity and structuring (see Nos 42-44), applies to:

- settlement firms;
- payment institutions;
- clearing institutions;
- electronic money institutions;
- entities for risk acceptance;
- banks;
- credit unions;
- premium pension institutions; and
- insurers.

Additionally, only the core prudential rules, concerning minimum capital, solvency and liquidity (see Nos 45- 48), also apply to the following 'Part 4 undertakings':

- UCITS management companies having their seat in the Netherlands;
- AIFMs;
- investment firms having their seat in the Netherlands providing investment services or performing investment activities in the Netherlands;

However, the application of these rules may differ, such as the minimum capital requirements, which depend on the relevant investment services and activities. Also, the liquidity requirements only apply to investment firms that 'deal on own account' or 'underwrite or place financial instruments'.

- depositaries having their seat in the Netherlands; and
- pension custodians.

International sources (Basel III and CRD IV)

The prudential rules in the FSA for banks and investment firms follow from the CRD (a directive). In addition, prudential rules apply directly to these firms pursuant to the CRR (a regulation). These European rules are the European implementation of a set of global rules drawn up by the Bank for International Settlements with the aim of strengthening the regulation, supervision and risk management of banks, Basel III.

The rules included in Basel III are based on three 'pillars':

- **Pillar 1, minimum capital requirements**: this pillar contains the strict quantitative requirements, such as the minimum capital requirements and the leverage ratio (see No 45 and 46).
- **Pillar 2, risk management and supervision**: this pillar contains the assessment by both the bank and its regulator of the eligibility of the capital, and the possibility for the regulator to take measures (see No 15); and
- **Pillar 3, market discipline and transparency**: this pillar contains reporting requirements to the market on the risks the bank is exposed to.

In addition to these three pillars, Basel III also contains rules on the liquidity of banks (such as the liquidity ratio (see No 48)) and additional rules for global systemically important banks (G-SIBs).

39 *Group finance companies*

There is only one exemption to the licence obligation for banks (see No 28) and the rules in Part 3, namely for so-called '(group) finance companies' whose purpose is to finance (parts of) the group to which they belong (Art. 3:2 FSA). The use of this exemption is subject to the following requirements:

- the repayable funds (obtained from non-professional market participants and from outside a closed circle) must be obtained by means of the offering of securities 'in accordance with" the rules pursuant to the Prospectus Regulation, *e.g.* by means of the following:
  - an approved prospectus is generally available; or
  - an exemption applies (see No 79);
- the relevant finance company must arrange for:
  - an unconditional guarantee from its parent company;
  - a bank guarantee from a European licensed bank or a bank in a state as referred to in Art. 3 of the Designated States (FSA) Decree (including Canada, USA and Switzerland); or
  - a keep-well agreement with its parent company; and
- at least 95% of the funds obtained must be lent out within the group (Arts. 3:2(1) and 3:2(3) FSA).

In this context, a 'group' means the collectivity of a legal entity and its subsidiaries.

In addition, (unless the finance company has arranged for a bank guarantee) the parent company must:

- have consolidated equity that is of a positive value for the full duration of the guarantee.
  This requirement is also met with a consolidated equity with a value of only € 1, regardless of any poor creditworthiness of its parent company; and
- ensure that the finance company can always fulfil its obligations towards lenders (basically constituting a keep-well obligation) (Art. 3:2(2) FSA).

Finally, the following applies:

- no group company may extend loans outside the group unless such group company (which has borrowed funds from the finance company) is a European licensed bank or a bank having its seat in a state as referred to in Art. 3 of the Designated States (FSA) Decree (Art. 3:2(4) FSA); and
- the finance company must be able to demonstrate, on an ongoing basis, that it meets the 'core' requirements for the exemption (Art. 3:2(5) FSA).

Dispensation

DNB may grant dispensation from certain requirements (Art. 3:2(7) FSA).

40 The prohibition to obtain repayable funds

It is prohibited for any person in the Netherlands to obtain repayable funds from the public in the course of a business, to receive such funds or to have them at disposal (Art. 3:5 FSA). This prohibition's aim, just like Art. 2:11 FSA, which prohibits the practice of a banking business without a licence, is to protect creditors.

Art. 3:5 FSA consists of several elements that determine the scope of the prohibition. For a discussion on the elements 'in the course of a business', 'deposits or other repayable funds' and 'public', reference is made to Nos 8 and 28.

- in this context, '**in the Netherlands**' means (see No 23):
  - the funds are attracted from Dutch borrowers, regardless of where such borrower is located; and
  - the funds are attracted from the borrower located in the Netherlands, regardless of the identity of the borrower.
- in this context, '**to obtain**', '**to receive**' and '**to have at disposal**' mean the following:
  - The term 'obtain' exists of three successive 'phases'; first, the offering of the possibility to provide repayable funds, then the entering into an agreement in relation to such repayable funds and finally the actual receipt of such repayable funds.

It follows from case law that even if the borrower does not actively try to obtain funds, it may still concern 'obtaining' repayable funds (see Court of Roermond 30 July 2003, JOR 2003/236, with commentary from Grundmann-van de Krol). In addition, the Supreme Court has ruled that where the funds are ultimately not obtained and therefore only the possibility to provide such funds is offered, this also amounts to obtaining repayable funds (see Supreme Court 27 September 2011, RF 2012/7).

  - 'Receiving' refers to the receipt of repayable funds and entering into the obligation to repay these repayable funds, for example through the issue of securities, the conclusion of loan agreements, the transfer of debt, the transfer of contracts or equivalents thereof. Therefore, the definition of this term terms overlaps with the definition of the term 'obtaining'.

- Having funds 'at its disposal' means that the borrower will have these funds in its possession for some time after it has obtained them. The 'having at its disposal' is therefore an ongoing event (even if the relevant funds are on-lent by the acquirer).

Statutory exemptions

Statutory exemptions apply to:

- licensed banks in the EEA;
- national, regional and local authorities;
- obtaining the repayable funds by means of offering securities in accordance with the Prospectus Regulation (see Nos 39 and 79);
- entities for risk acceptance; and
- credit unions having their seat in the Netherlands (Art. 3:5(2) FSA).

Exemption Regulation

Exempt are:

- bailiffs and notaries;
- foundations for third party monies;
- issuers of bearer securities as part of a sales transaction;
- payment service providers as referred to in Art. 1a FSA Exemption Regulation;
- trust offices with special accounts;
- foundations exclusively operating for trust offices;

- administrators as referred to in the Debt Restructuring (Natural Persons) Act; and
- persons obtaining repayable funds via crowdfunding; as referred to in Article 2a(2) of the MCSD (Art. 3:5(3) and Art. 19 to 24b FSA Exemption Regulation).

Dispensation

DNB may grant a dispensation (Art. 3:5(4) FSA) under certain conditions (see Arts. 27-34 PFSD).

41 The prohibition to use the word 'bank'

Any person that is not a licensed bank is prohibited to use the word 'bank', translations or forms thereof, in their name or in the conduct of their business (Art. 3:7 of the FSA). The rationale for this being that public must be able to trust that those who use the word bank are subject to strict banking supervision. However, the word bank may be used if this is done in such a way that it is clear that the relevant user does not operate on the financial markets, for example the blood bank.

Statutory exemptions

Statutory exemptions apply to:
- financial institutions subject to supervision in the EEA;
- licensed banks seated in the EEA; and
- representative organisations of supervised banks or financial institutions (Art. 3:7(2) FSA).

Exemption Regulation

Exempt are:

- advance banks;
- municipal money-lending and debt counselling institutions;
- AIFs and UCITS of licensed banks in the EEA;
- securities investment systems and client money custodian institutions;
- subsidiaries of (and guaranteed by) licensed banks in the EEA; and
- brokers and intermediaries of licensed banks in the EEA (Arts. 26-31 FSA Exemption Regulation).

Dispensation

DNB may grant a dispensation (Art. 3:7(4) FSA).

42 *Suitability and trustworthiness*

For the sake of brevity, we refer to Nos 64 and 66 for the requirements regarding suitability and trustworthiness (Arts. 3:8 FSA and 3:9 FSA), which apply *mutatis mutandis*. One deviation concerns Art. 3:8(3) in relation to banks (see Art. 4:9.0a FSA for (significant) investment firms). This article concerns the implementation of a provision under CRD relating to the 'good governance' of significant banks (and investment firms).

Significant banks (and investment firms) are subject to the requirement that board members may not fulfil more than the maximum number of allowed board positions. This requirement may overlap with the rules with respect to this included in the first and second paragraphs of Arts. 2:132a, 2:142a, 2:242a and 2:252a of the DCC, provided that Art. 3:8(3)(b) of the FSA disapplies these articles of the DCC in relation to significant banks (see No 22 for the term 'significant banks'). CRD applies a maximum of four board positions (Art. 91 CRD), relative to the maximum of five board positions under the DCC.

43 *Integrity policy*

For the sake of brevity, we refer to No 67 in relation to the required integrity policy that a financial firm must have in place, which applies *mutatis mutandis*. Please find the minimum requirements in Art. 10 PRD.

Numbered accounts

Banks are also subject to the requirement that their policy covers 'numbered accounts' (Art. 14(6) PRD). Numbered accounts often aim to protect the privacy and security of the clients involved. Despite these legitimate interests, banks must, in principle, be restrictive in opening such accounts for clients.

In order to meet both clients' interests and to accommodate the desired level of transparency, DNB has issued the Numbered Accounts (FSA) Regulation.

44 *Structuring and organisation*

Four-eye principle and control structure

The daily policy of (amongst others) a bank must be determined by at least two natural persons who perform their activities from the Netherlands (Art. 3:15 FSA). In addition, there are requirements regarding the structure of control (Art. 3:16 FSA), for which we refer to No 68, which apply *mutatis mutandis*.

Organisation of business operations

For the sake of brevity, we refer to No 68 in relation to the required organization of business operations (Art. 3:17 FSA).

The general aspects and the integrity aspects apply *mutatis mutandis* (Art. 3:17(2)(a) and (b) FSA, and Chapter 3 and Section 4.1 PRD). Furthermore, some additional requirements are explained below in relation to:

- general aspects;
- integrity aspects; and
- prudential aspects.

General aspects

Conflict of interest. Financial firms must have in place policies to prevent conflicts of the private interests of:

- policymakers (see No 66);
- group directors;
- members of the supervisory board (the supervisory board or similar bodies); and
- other employees or persons that, on the basis of the instructions of the relevant financial firm, perform activities for this firm, affecting the firm's and the client's interests (Art. 11(1) PRD),

because this:

- may have a negative impact on both the clients of the relevant financial firm and the financial firm itself; and
- may damage the public confidence in the financial markets as a whole.

The financial firm must have in place procedures and measures in place to ensure that if financial services are offered to policymakers and group directors, such provision must:

- be on staff terms;

This concerns both the financial conditions, such as pricing and discounts, and other conditions, such as maturities, (re)payment obligations and the provision of collateral in relation to the income of the person to whom, for example, a credit is granted.

- take place in the ordinary course of business; and
- in each case only may take place after approval by the supervisory board (Art. 11(2) and (3) PRD).

If:

- the relevant written staff conditions are not used or are deviated from (e.g. with respect to the amount of credit); or
- in the case of the provision of services to members of the supervisory board or their family members, or to family members of policymakers and group directors, this may only take place within the ordinary course of business and must be subject to usual commercial conditions and granting of security (Art. 11(4) and (5) PRD).

Commercial conditions are regarded as conditions that apply to customers in the ordinary course of business, regardless of whether the relevant financial firm has a profit motive. If services are provided exclusively to directors and group directors and therefore not to third parties, then conditions that are in line with the market conditions must be applied.

Back-to-back loans. Banks must have in place a policy on the granting of back-to-back loans (see Art. 1 PRD) in order to prevent possible abuse (Art. 15 PRD). On the basis of this policy, it must be clear to both employees and clients when such a loan is granted and when it is not.

Two conditions apply to the granting of back-to-back loans:

- The bank must examine whether the purpose of the loan is legitimate; and

This means that the bank must examine whether the relevant transaction is used to launder money or whether it is used for other objectionable practices, such as illegal tax structures.

- At the moment the relevant loan agreement is concluded, the essential collateral provided must be specified as well.

Essential collateral is considered as the collateral without which the loan agreement would not have been concluded and which serves to secure the payment of the principal amount, interest and costs of the loan granted. Such collateral may be provided in various ways. However, such collateral is often provided in the form of a deposit, a guarantee or financial assets held in a depot.

Integrity aspects

Governance. The governance arrangements that banks must have in place in relation to the management board and supervision thereof, are subject to a number of requirements (Art. 17c PRD and Art. 88 CRD). The management board and the supervisory board must:

- bear the overall responsibility for the firm, approve its strategic objectives, its risk strategy and its internal governance;
- ensure the integrity of the accounting and financial reporting systems;
- monitor the implementation of the above; and
- monitor and assess the effectiveness of the firm's governance arrangements and take appropriate steps to address any deficiencies.

The chairperson of the supervisory board may not simultaneously be the chief executive officer of the firm.

A bank that is significant in terms of its size, internal organisation and the nature, scope and complexity of its activities must have in place a nomination committee. The tasks of such nomination committee include:
- drawing up job profiles for vacancies for the management board;
- selecting candidates; and
- ensuring that the composition of the management body is sufficiently diverse and includes the right mix of knowledge, skills and experience (Art. 17c(2) PRD).

Adequate segregation of duties. The tasks, powers and responsibilities of both persons and bodies must be allocated in such way that it reduces the risk of the occurrence of errors and of the improper use of assets or data (Art. 18 PRD). Furthermore, it must be prevented that functions include powers that would enable a single person (without any system of control) to enter into, authorise, process and settle transactions or commitments, and to have free access to assets or to manipulate financial and/or other data.

Information systems. A financial firm must have in place an information system that enables effective control of the business processes and risks. Furthermore, such system must meet internal and external information needs (Art. 20 PRD). The automated data must always be available.

For example:
Backups (safety copies), recovery measures and an emergency plan that are regularly updated and tested on proper functioning.

Prudential aspects

The prudential aspects entail that the business operations must be structured in order to ensure the soundness of the financial firm (Art. 3:17(2) (c) FSA). For example, this could include:

- procedures for the management of financial risks (market risk, credit risk, insurance risk and liquidity risk) and other risks that may deteriorate the soundness of the firm;
- procedures relating to the maintenance of financial safeguards (including liquidity and solvency requirements); or
- procedures relating to the establishment, maintenance and operation of a recovery plan, *i.e.* a preparatory crisis plan that provides for the measures as referred to in Art. 3A:2 FSA that enable the firm to restore its financial position after a deterioration thereof.

In addition to the 'Part 3 companies', the following 'Part 4 companies' must also comply with these rules (Art. 3:17 (3) FSA):

- UCITS management companies seated in the Netherlands;
- investment firms seated in the Netherlands that operate in the Netherlands;

- depositaries seated in the Netherlands; and
- Dutch AIFMs.

Risk management. Depending on the type and size of the financial firm, it is exposed to different risks. Therefore, financial firms must conduct a policy that is aimed at managing the relevant risks (Art. 23 PRD). The risk management must ensure that the overall risk profile of the relevant financial firm is proportionate to its financial resources, in order to ensure the ongoing adequate capitalisation of the financial firm. The relevant risks are considered to include (Art. 23(2) PRD):

- **Concentration risk**: *the risks arising from the number of claims to the same counterparties, groups of connected counterparties and counterparties that operate in the same economic sector or are from the same geographical region. Furthermore, it includes the risks that are connected with the same activities or commodities and the application of techniques to reduce credit risk (in particular the large indirect credit risks).*
- **Credit risk**: the existing or future threat to the firm's equity and financial performance as a result of a counterparty's non-performance of its financial or other contractual obligation to the firm, including the possibility of restrictions or impediments on the transfers of payments from abroad.
- **Liquidity risk**: the existing or future threat to the firm's equity and financial performance as a result of the possibility that at a given point in time, it will no longer be able to meet its short-term obligations without incurring unacceptable costs.
- **Market risk**: the existing or future threat to the firm's equity and financial performance as a result of movements in market prices. Market risk includes price risk, interest rate risk and currency risk on and outside the firm's trading book.

- **Operational risk**: the risk to incur losses that arise from inadequate or failed internal procedures and systems, which may also arise as a result of external events, including legal risks. An important part of the operational risk is IT risk, which can be described as the existing or future threat to the firm's equity and financial performance as a result of an inadequate strategy and policy or shortcomings in the technology applied and/or the use of data processing and communication, which may translate into strategic, policy, security, management and continuity risks.
- **Interest rate risk**: the current or future threat to the firm's equity and financial performance as a result of potential fluctuations in interest rates.
- **Residual risk**: the risk that the applied and recognized techniques for the reduction of credit risk are less effective than expected.
- **Insurance risk**: the existing or future credit risk threat to the firm's equity and financial performance as a result of inadequate tariffs, tariff principles, insurance conditions or bases for determining the technical provisions, or as a result of insufficiently controlled acceptance and reinsurance measures, as a result of which existing or future obligations may not adequately be paid with by the collected premia or investment income.

In order to ensure proper compliance with the financial firm's policy that is aimed at managing the abovementioned risks, such policy must be laid down in procedures and measures. These procedures and measures must be integrated into the financial firm's business operations, as a result of which they are applied by employees on a day-to-day basis (Art. 23(3) PRD).

Financial firms must set limits on the risks to be taken and monitor potential exceeding of these limits. Additionally, they must have in place procedures and measures to control emergency situations.

For example:
The procedures on dealing with liquidity shortfalls or the collection or restructuring of outstanding loans.

The procedures and measures must be aligned with the nature, size, risk profile and complexity of the financial firm (Art. 23(4) PRD).

A financial firm must carry out independent risk management of which a part consists of the risk analysis: systematic measurement, monitoring, documenting and reporting of the risks incurred (Art. 23(6) PRD). The purpose of this analysis is to understand the risks to which the financial firm is exposed and to determine whether these are in line with the strategy and policy principles. Independent risk management means that the risk analysis is not influenced by commercial or other interests. Therefore, the risk analysis must be carried out, and the results must be reported outside the control of the management that is responsible for the firm's financial performance.

Dealing with risks. Additionally, banks, CRR investment firms and clearing institutions must deal with and take into account different types of risks in accordance with Arts. 79-87 CRD (Art. 23a PRD) in the policies, procedures and measures that are drawn up by them in accordance with the above. For the most part, this concerns the same risks as set out above, plus the securitisation risk (Art. 82 CRD) and the risk of excessive leverage (Art. 87 CRD).

Involvement of the management board and the supervisory board. The management board and the supervisory board of a bank, CRR-investment firm or a clearing institution must be closely and actively involved in the risk management of the firm (Art. 23b PRD). For example, they (in their own role) have to adopt, on a case-by-case basis, an overall strategy and policies in this field, periodically review these and monitor their implementation.

If the firm is significant in terms of its size, internal organisation and the nature, scope and complexity of its activities, it should establish a risk committee to:

- advise the management board and supervisory board on their risk appetite and risk strategy; and
- assist the management board and supervisory board in monitoring the implementation of the firm's risk strategy (Art. 23b(3) PRD).

Furthermore, it must be ensured that the management board and supervisory board are at all times properly informed about the firm's risk situation, the risk management function and about any advice from external experts.

Whistle-blower scheme. Banks and investment firms must have in place procedures that enable employees to internally report breaches of prudential requirements (Art. 23i PRD). A specific, independent and autonomous channel must be available for such reporting. Furthermore, it must also be ensured that employees who report such breaches are adequately protected against retaliation or any other form of unfair treatment.

45 Minimum capital

Financial firms are required to hold a minimum amount of capital (Art. 3:53 FSA). Different requirements apply to each type of financial firm in relation to:

- the amount; and
- the composition (which assets are eligible to be included in the calculation of capital for these purposes) (Chapter 9 PRD).

The amounts

In principle, the minimum amounts of capital that apply are the following:

- for a bank (which does not mainly conduct the business of the provision of investment services or the performance of investment activities): € 5 million;
- for an AIFM: € 125,000;
- for a UCITS management company: € 125,000;
- for an investment company or a UCITS company that does not have an external manager: € 300,000;
- for an investment firm, depending on:
- the investment services being provided, or the investment activities being performed;
- whether activities are carried out abroad;
- whether it is permitted to hold clients' monies or financial instruments; or
- whether a professional liability insurance has been concluded: € 25,000 and € 730,000 (Art. 48 PRD).

For an insurer (not being an insurer with limited risks), the minimum capital requirement pursuant to Art. 129 Solvency II Directive applies, taking into account Title I of Chapter VII of the

Delegated Regulation Solvency II (Regulation (EU) 2015/35) (Art. 49 PRD). Consequently, the following floors apply:
- to a non-life insurer: € 2,200,000;
- to a life insurer: € 3,200,000; and
- to a reinsurer: € 3,200,000.

The composition

The composition is as follows. For:
- a bank;
- an AIFM;
- a UCITS management company; or
- an investment firm,

the minimum capital must consist of exclusively one or more of the following 'common equity tier 1 items' (see No 46):
- capital instruments (provided that the conditions laid down in Art. 28 CRR are met);
- the share premium accounts related to those the capital instruments;
- retained earnings;
- accumulated other comprehensive income; and
- other reserves (Art. 50 PRD).

For an insurer, the minimum capital and reserves must consist of exclusively one or more of the following 'core tier 1 items':
- the excess of assets over liabilities; or
- subordinated liabilities (Art. 52 PRD).

46 *Solvency and financial position*

In addition to the minimum capital requirement, a solvency requirement applies pursuant to which financial firms must maintain sufficient equity relative to the risks of losses on their receivables and investments (assets) (Art. 3:57 FSA). After all, losses on assets must be deducted from equity.

For banks, the solvency requirement amounts to a simple calculation: the own funds ('regulatory capital I') must have a value at least equal to a certain percentage of the risk-weighted assets ('risk exposure'), which percentage is 8% (Art. 59(3) PRD and Art. 92 CRR). This 'total capital ratio' is expressed in the following formula:

$$\text{minimum own funds} \leq \frac{\text{regulatory capital}}{\text{total risk exposure}}$$

In practice, banks intend to be better capitalised than is required on basis of the solvency requirement.

Regulatory capital

Regulatory capital includes only capital instruments that may function as buffer against losses, such as shares and share like instruments (including subordinated loans/bonds and instruments having the characteristics of both equity and debt, also being referred to as 'hybrid instruments'). After all, these capital instruments contribute to the protection of creditors and the financial stability by reducing the risks of bankruptcy.

Regulatory capital consists of two components (Art. 1 PRD and Art. 72 CRR):

- Tier 1 capital, which in turn consists of the sum of Common Equity Tier 1 capital and the Additional Tier 1 capital (Art. 25 CRR); and
- Tier 2 capital.

Common Equity Tier 1 (CET 1) capital is of the highest quality and most loss-absorbing capital. It mainly consists of the following components:
- capital instruments;
- reserves; and
- retained earnings (Art. 26 CRR).

In order to qualify as CET1 capital, capital instruments must meet thirteen cumulative requirements (Art. 28 CRR). Pursuant to Dutch law, only shares will qualify as CET1 capital.

On the basis of Art. 26 CRR, EBA regularly publishes a list of capital instruments that are considered as Common Equity Tier 1 instruments in various member states.

Additional Tier 1 (AT 1) capital is the second most loss-absorbing capital after CET 1 capital and mainly consists of hybrid capital instruments not qualifying as shares or of Tier 2 items (Art. 51 CRR). These capital instruments combine the characteristics of both equity and debt. They must meet sixteen cumulative requirements, including the requirement that they must be perpetual and that the provisions governing the relevant instruments provide that the principal amount of the instrument is written down (temporary or permanent) or that the instruments can be converted into CET 1 capital, if the CET 1 ratio of the relevant issuing firm falls below a predetermined minimum level (Art. 52 CRR).

Because of this conditional convertibility, AT 1 capital instruments are also being referred to as contingent convertible securities ('CoCos').

Tier 2 capital is also loss absorbing, but less than CET 1 and AT 1 and mainly consists of capital instruments (other than Tier 1 capital instruments), highly subordinated loans and debt instruments (Art. 62 CRR). The capital instruments must meet fourteen cumulative requirements, including the requirement that they must have an original maturity of at least five years (Art. 63 CRR).

Deduction

Certain items are excluded or deducted from the available Tier 1 capital and Tier 2 capital (Arts. 50, 61 and 71 CRR), including:

- goodwill and other intangible assets;
- the deferred tax assets that rely on future profitability;
- defined benefit pension fund assets that are on the relevant firms balance sheet;
- holdings of own CET1 instruments; and
- certain holdings in certain other financial firms ('financial sector entities') (Art. 36(1) CRR).

Capital ratios

- total regulatory capital must have a value of at least 8% of the value of the risk-weighted assets,
- the Tier 1 capital must have a value of at least 6% of the value of the risk-weighted assets; and
- the Common Equity Tier 1 capital must have a value of at least 4.5% of the risk-weighted assets (Art. 92 CRR).

In addition, banks have to maintain their capital buffer in the form of Common Equity Tier 1 capital (see No 47).

Risk-weighted assets/risk exposure

The framework for the risk-weighting of credit ('exposure') provides for two methods:

- **Standardised method**: this is the simplest method used by the majority of smaller banks. This method applies risk weights based on (i) the exposure class to which the relevant risk exposure is assigned to (Art. 112 CRR) and (ii) the credit rating category in which the relevant risk exposure falls (which is aligned with the credit ratings of credit rating agencies; the lower the rating, the higher the risk weight). *The advantage of this method is that it seems to create a level playing field as a result of which banks may easily be compared by outsiders. However, the disadvantage of this method it does not take into account bank specific risks.*
- **Internal modelling method, also being referred to as the Internal Ratings Based Approach (IRB), which is subdivided into 'Foundation IRB' and 'Advanced IRB'**: this method may only be used with the consent of DNB (Art. 143 CRR). *The advantage of this method is that the bank is allowed to include bank-specific risks in the calculations. The disadvantage is that the calculations of the different banks are more difficult to compare.*

Under the standardised method, credit risk is calculated by multiplying (a) the value of each exposure (consisting of an asset or off-balance sheet item) by (b) a specified risk weight (expressed as a percentage) that has been assigned to each exposure. The exposure value of a loan is equal to its balance sheet value. At least 8% of this risk-weighted exposure value ('risk exposure') must be held as regulatory capital.

For example:
Bank X granted a loan of € 1,000 to Firm Y. Firm Y has an A+ rating from Standard & Poor's. It follows from Art. 122 CRR, which regards the exposures to corporates, that a risk weight of 50% applies. Consequently, the risk-weighted exposure value is € 500, which means that Bank X must hold € 40 (i.e. 8% of € 500) as regulatory capital.

47 Capital buffer

Banks and investment firms that underwrite, place financial instruments on a commitment basis or deal on own account must maintain a capital buffer in excess of the standard solvency requirements (Art. 3:62a FSA). If applicable, the capital buffer is the sum of:

- the capital conservation buffer of 2.5% (Art. 105a PRD) (which actually leads to an increase of the solvency requirement from 8% to 10.5%);
- the countercyclical capital buffer between 0 and 2.5% (which covers the risks arising from a credit cycle (Art. 105b PRD); and
- the highest percentage of the buffer requirement for systematically relevant institutions between 1 and 3.5% (which covers the risks arising from non-cyclical (macro-prudential) long-term systemic risks; Art. 105d PRD) and the systemic risk buffer (which covers the risk that a bank poses to the stability of the financial system; Art. 105e PRD).

Banks are not allowed to pay distributions if this would result in non-compliance with the requirement to hold an adequate amount of Common Equity Tier 1 capital (Art. 3:62b FSA). If a bank already holds an insufficient capital buffer, it is not allowed to:

- pay distributions if this would negatively affect the Common Equity Tier 1 capital;
- to grant or pay variable bonusses; and
- make payments on Additional Tier 1 instruments.

In such a case, a bank must also submit a capital conservation plan to DNB. In this plan, the bank must indicate how it will recover its capital buffer to the required level within a reasonable period of time.

48 Liquidity

Banks must ensure that they have sufficient liquidity (Art. 3:63 FSA and Part 6 CRR). Liquidity regards the availability of financial resources in order to ensure that the firm is able to meet its short-term obligations. The rationale being that despite the fact that the bank has a strong capital position, it may get into problems if many creditors retrieve their money in a short period of time. For example, this may be the result of a so-called bank run, which refers to the situation in which many deposit holders (and others) withdraw their money from the bank, because they are concerned that the bank may default in the near future. The liquidity requirement intends to prevent that a bank gets into problems if such scenario occurs.

A financial firm's liquidity position (also being referred to as the liquidity coverage ratio, **LCR**) is calculated by dividing the available liquidity (the liquidity buffer) by the expected needed liquidity (net liquidity outflows). The quotient (result) is the liquidity coverage ratio. If this ratio is at least 100%, the bank meets with the liquidity requirement (Art. 4(2) Delegated Regulation (EU) No 2015/61, **Delegated Regulation on Liquidity**).

This calculation is expressed in the following formula:

$$\frac{\text{liquidity buffer}}{\begin{array}{c}\text{total net liquidity outflows}\\ \text{(total outflows - total inflows)}\\ \text{over a 30 calendar day period}\end{array}} \geq \text{liquidity coverage ratio}$$

The net liquidity outflows is calculated by deducting the expected total liquidity inflows from the total liquidity outflows (Art. 3(7) Delegated Regulation on Liquidity). This calculation takes into account the net liquidity outflows for the next 30 calendar days as if turbulent market conditions were present during this period ('a stress period').

The liquidity buffer is calculated by aggregating all high-quality liquid assets (Art. 3(3) Delegated Regulation on Liquidity). In this calculation, the market value of the relevant liquid assets must be used as a starting point. Subsequently, such market value must be reduced in accordance with pre-determined haircuts (Art. 9 Delegated Regulation on Liquidity). Such haircuts are allocated on the basis of the ease with which the relevant assets can be converted into cash.

49 *Technical provisions*

Instead of the liquidity requirements (see No 48), insurers are subject to requirements with regard to technical provisions (Art. 3:67 FSA). The rationale being that the core business and the structure of the balance sheet of insurers differ from those of banks and investment firms. A characterising element of an insurance is the 'probability element': it is unknown if, and if so, how much the insurer will have to pay out.

Technical provisions are considered to be a reservation of an amount that is a reasonable estimation of the insurer's (future) expected payment obligations.

The value of the technical provisions must be at least equal to the amount that an insurer would have to pay if it would immediately transfer its insurance obligations to another insurer (Art. 3:67(2) FSA).

The PRD lays down rules regarding the calculation of the technical provisions (Art. 12.1 PRD):

- the insurer's (future) payment obligations must be calculated on the basis of (among other things) historical data and adequate prudent models;
- the insurer must, at all times, be able to demonstrate the appropriateness of its technical provisions, the applicability and relevance of the methods applied, and the adequacy of the underlying statistical data used, if DNB requests to do so (Art. 84 Solvency II Directive);
- insurers are required to calculate the technical provisions in accordance with Arts. 76-83 and 192 Solvency II Directive, which are further elaborated upon in Title I, Chapter III Solvency II Regulation (Art. 114 PRD); and
- the valuation of the technical provisions entails a best estimate plus a risk margin. Such risk margin aims to compensate for making available the insurer's own equity.

Additionally, the PRD includes certain investment rules, which elaborate upon Art. 3:267h(2) FSA (Art. 12.2 PRD). These rules apply to all assets, including assets that form the insurer's equity. The starting principle for insurers' investment policies is the so-called 'prudent person principle' (Art. 132 of Directive Solvency II). Pursuant to this principle, an insurer may only invest in assets and instruments whose risks it is able to properly identify, measure and manage in such a manner as to ensure the security, quality, liquidity and the profitability of the portfolio as a whole. Furthermore, pursuant to the prudent person principle investments must be properly diversified in such a way as to avoid excessive reliance on any asset, issuer or geographical area (Art. 132(4) Solvency II Directive).

Dutch insurers must comply with the investment rules of the Solvency II Directive and the Solvency II Regulation (particularly Title I, Chapter VIII) (Art. 118 PRD).

For insurers with limited risks, a less extensive regime regarding the technical provisions applies (Art. 117 PRD). However, also this type of insurers must comply with the prudent person principle and with the directive and regulation in this respect (Art. 120 PRD).

The statutory balance sheet of an insurer that complies with the rules of Book 2 of the DCC differs from balance sheets that comply with the Solvency II regime.

50 *Qualifying holdings in and by financial firms*

In a financial firm

It is prohibited to hold, acquire or increase a qualifying holding in certain financial firms, unless a declaration of no objection (DNO) has been obtained from DNB or, in the case of a bank, the ECB (Art. 3:95 FSA). The relevant financial firms are:

- clearing and settlement institutions having their seat in the Netherlands;
- banks having their seat Netherlands;
- UCITS management companies having their seat in the Netherlands;
- investment firms seated in the Netherlands;
- entities for risk acceptance;
- premium pension institutions having their seat in the Netherlands;
- insurers having their seat in Netherlands;
- payment institutions; and
- electronic money institutions.

The term 'qualifying holding' refers to:

- an (in)direct holding of at least 10% of the capital or the voting rights; and
- a level of control comparable to this (Art. 1:1 FSA).

Furthermore, in principle, a new DNO must be applied for, if the relevant holding is increased to 20%, 33%, 50% and 100% (Art. 3:95 FSA and Art. 3:103 FSA). If a holding is increased, but these thresholds are not exceeded, there is no need to apply for a new DNO.

When applying for a DNO, the following information must be submitted to DNB:

- an indication of the size of the qualifying holding;
- information on the basis of which DNB is able to assess whether the applicant complies with the rules of the FSA regarding the trustworthiness of the applicant that by virtue of the relevant qualifying holding will be able to (co-)determine the day-to-day policy of the relevant financial firm; and
- documents setting out the financial position and the legal group structure of the applicant (Art. 138 PRD).

Assessment criteria

After an application, DNB (or the ECB) will issue a DNO, unless:

- the trustworthiness of the applicant or of the persons who, by virtue of the qualifying holding, will be able to (co-)determine the day-to-day policy of the relevant firm is not beyond reasonable doubt;
- the suitability of the applicant, also considering its reputation, or of the policy makers is not beyond doubt;
- the financial soundness of the applicant is not guaranteed;
- as a result of the acquisition of the qualifying holding, the relevant financial firm will no longer be able to comply with prudential requirements of the FSA;
- there are good grounds to assume that money laundering or terrorist financing play a role in the prospective acquisition or increase the risks of such activities being involved; or
- the applicant has submitted incomplete or incorrect information (Art. 3:100 FSA).

By a financial firm (bank or insurer)

In certain cases, banks and insurers seated in the Netherlands must also apply to DNB for a DNO (Art. 3:96 FSA and 3:97 FSA).

A bank must obtain a DNO before it:

- acquires or increases a qualifying holding in a:
  - bank, investment firm or insurer seated in a non-member state;
  - a financial institution to which no certificate of supervised status has been granted; or
  - other firms.
- acquires (indirectly) the whole or a significant part of the assets and liabilities of another firm;
- enters into a legal merger with another firm;
- initiates a financial or corporate reorganisation; or
- appoints a managing partner (Art. 3:96(1) FSA).

A DNO is only required if:

- the holding in, or the legal merger with, concerns a financial firm with a balance sheet total of;
- regarding non-financial firms, it concerns a purchase amount of; or
- the assets and liabilities to be acquired amount to a total amount of

more than 1% of the bank's own balance sheet (Art. 3:96(1)) FSA).

An insurer must obtain a DNO if it intends to:

- reduce its equity by redemption or purchase of its own shares; or
- distribute dividends, and

it does not meet the solvency Capital Requirement at the time of reduction or in case it is likely that the insurer will be unable to satisfy this solvency capital requirement within the next twelve months (Art. 3:97 FSA).

Assessment criteria

After an application, DNB will issue a DNO , unless:

- this act (might) conflict with the solvency capital requirements that apply to the relevant bank or insurer;
- this act might otherwise conflict with a sound and prudent conduct of business; and
- this act (might) lead to an undesirable development of the financial sector (Art. 3:101 FSA).

51 *Measures in the event of breaches of prudential rules*

If a bank or investment firm fails to comply with CRR (or Part 3.5.1 of the FSA), if there are indications that it is likely that a bank or investment firm may no longer comply within twelve months, or if the periodic review indicates that sound risk management and sound risk coverage are insufficiently guaranteed, DNB may take certain measures (Art. 3:111a(1) FSA). These measures may include:

- prescribing that the relevant firm must comply with a higher solvency or liquidity level (see Nos. 46 and 48) than is required under CRR or the FSA;
- prescribing that the relevant firm must amend its business operations (*e.g.* its remuneration policy in respect of variable pay) and strategies, and its procedures and measures for risk management;

- prescribing that the relevant firm must carry out a facilities policy;
- imposing restrictions or prohibitions on dividend payments;
- prescribing that the relevant firm must use its net profit to strengthen its solvency; or
- requiring that certain regulated information is submitted more frequently to DNB, that more information is submitted to DNB or that certain information is published by the relevant firm.

Periodically, banks and investment firms must assess their capital and liquidity positions and the adequacy thereof (also being referred to as the Internal Capital Adequacy Assessment Process (**ICAAP**) and the Internal Liquidity Adequacy Assessment Process (**ILAAP**) (Art. 3:17(2)(c) FSA). On the basis of DNB's assessment of the ICAAP and ILAAP (also being referred to as the Supervisory Review and Evaluation Process (**SREP**) (Art. 3:18a FSA)), DNB may require a bank to comply with a higher solvency or liquidity requirement than required under the FSA (Art. 3:111a(2)(a) FSA). In certain situations, DNB is even obliged to prescribe such higher solvency or liquidity requirement (Art. 3:111a(3) FSA).

52 *Transfer of portfolio by insurers*

Insurers seated the Netherlands

Life insurers (Art. 3:112 FSA) having their seat in the Netherlands require DNB's consent for the transfer of rights and obligations under a:

- life insurance agreement, that is concluded by a branch located in a member state, to an insurer seated in another member state (sub a);

- life insurance agreement, that is concluded by an insurer seated in the Netherlands, to an insurer seated in another member state (sub b); or
- life insurance agreement, that is concluded by a branch located in another member state, to an insurer seated in a non-member state (sub c).

DNB's consent to life insurers is not required if the transfer takes place at the request of the policyholder (Art. 3:112(3) FSA).

Non-life insurers can affect the transfer in two ways:
- with the cooperation of the relevant policyholders (via the assignment of debt (Art. 6:155 DCC) and contract assignment (Art. 6:159 DCC); or
- without the cooperation of the relevant policyholders, but instead with the consent of DNB (Art. 3:114 FSA).

If the latter variant is chosen, the procedure is the same as the one for a life insurer.

Insurers seated in another member state

The transfer can take place with the consent of DNB if:
- the law of the relevant member state does not provide for an approval procedure; and
- the relevant insurance agreements are concluded by the Dutch branch of the relevant insurer and the rights and obligations thereunder are transferred to an insurer seated in a non-member state (Art. 3:122 FSA).

DNB only grants its consent if the home state regulator agrees with the transfer.

Insurers seated in a non-member state

The consent of DNB is required for life insurance agreements (Art. 3:126(1) FSA) and may be granted for non-life insurance agreements (Art. 3:122 FSA):

- in the event of a transfer of an insurance to an insurer seated in a member state; or
- in the event of a transfer of an insurance to an insurer seated in a non-member state, in the course of business conducted from a Dutch branch.

DNB only grants its consent if the life insurer or non-life insurer complies with the solvency capital requirement, also in view of the intended transfer, and if DNB has no objections to the transfer (Art. 3:118 FSA).

53 *Recovery plan*

Within two months after it has been established that the solvency capital requirement is not being met by a Dutch insurer (Art. 3:57(4) FSA), such insurer must submit a recovery plan to DNB for approval (Art. 3:135(1) FSA).

Such recovery plan must include:

- the expected management costs, particularly the current general costs and commissions;
- a forecast of revenues and expenses, in respect of the insurance business, the accepted reinsurance agreements and the assignment of reinsurance agreements;
- a statement of the expected balance sheet position;

- an estimate of the financial resources available to cover the technical provisions and the solvency and minimum capital requirements; and
- the overall reinsurance policy (Chapter 3 SPMD which refers to Art. 142(1) Solvency II Directive).

The insurer must take the necessary measures to ensure that, within six months after the establishment as referred to above, the own funds eligible to cover the solvency capital requirement are brought back to the required level or to adjust its risk profile in such a way that this requirement is met (Art. 3:135(3) FSA). DNB may extend this period by three months (Art. 3:135(4) FSA).

54 Investor compensation scheme and deposit guarantee scheme

Investor compensation scheme

The investor compensation scheme is based on a European directive: the Investor Compensation Schemes Directive. This directive has been implemented in the FSA and SPMD.

The purpose of the Investor Compensation Scheme (**ICS**) is to compensate persons who have entrusted monies or financial instruments to an investment firm, a bank or a financial institution in relation to the provision of an investment service or an ancillary service in the event that the relevant institutions are no longer able to meet their obligations (Art. 3:259(1) FSA).

The maximum amount that can be compensated under the ICS is € 20,000 per person (Art. 26(4) SPMD).

The following financial firms participate in the ICS:

- banks that have a banking licence granted by DNB and are permitted to provide investment services;
- investment firms providing investment services;
- AIFMs and UCITS management companies licensed by the AFM, provided that the AIFMs are allowed to provide the investment services as referred to in Art. 2:67a(2) FSA and the UCITS management companies are allowed to provide individual portfolio management services;
- financial institutions that hold a certificate of supervised status, which are allowed to provide investment services; and
- other institutions, such as certain financial firms having their seat in the Netherlands with a branch in another member state and, where applicable, Dutch branches of banks and investment firms (Art. 8 SPMD).

Dutch branches of banks and investment firms established in the EU and Norway, Iceland and Liechtenstein are subject to their home country ICS. However, they may opt for additional participation in the Dutch ICS if their own ICS has a relatively limited coverage.

DNB executes the Dutch ICS. This means that DNB activates the system if it establishes a firm's inability to pay which falls within scope of the ICS. In such case, DNB publishes, amongst others on its website and via advertisements, how investors can claim compensation under the ICS. Furthermore, DNB is responsible for determining and executing payments under the ICS (Art. 24-27 SPMD).

The ICS is financed in two ways; in the event of inability to pay by:

- a bank which also provides investment services, the amount that will be paid out under the ICS will be apportioned to other banks according to a procedure similar to the allocation procedure under the Deposit Guarantee Scheme; or
- a financial firm not being a bank (such as an investment firm), the ICS is financed by an investor compensation fund. This fund is financed by mandatory annual contributions from institutions participating in the ICS. Such annual contribution consist of a fixed levy and a variable levy, the latter depends on the number of retail clients of the investment firm (Art. 29 SPMD).

Deposit Guarantee Scheme

In order to give account holders of a bank some certainty that they will get their money back in the event a bank fails, the Deposit Guarantee Schemes Directive (2014/49/EU) introduced a system of Deposit Guarantee Schemes across the EU. The purpose of the Deposit Guarantee Scheme (**DGS**) is to compensate deposit holders in the event that a bank is unable to meet its obligations arising from claims on deposits (Art. 3:259(2) FSA).

The maximum amount that can be compensated under the DGS is € 100,000 per account holder per bank (Art. 29.02 SPMD).

The DGS applies to the following types of banks:

- banks that are licensed on the basis of Art. 2:11 FSA (Art. 3:258 FSA), with the exception of branches in non-member states;
- licensed banks seated in the EEA that provide their services in the Netherlands via a branch (Art. 3:266(1)(b) FSA) and that have opted for additional participation in the DGS; and

- after the approval of DNB, banks seated in non-member states that provide their services in the Netherlands via a branch (Art. 3:267(2) FSA) (Art. 29.01(1) SPMD).

The DGS does not apply to:

- deposits of:
  - banks, provided that it concerns deposits that are held by a bank on its own behalf and for its own account;
  - financial institutions;
  - investment firms;
  - deposit holders who have not identified themselves in accordance with Art. 4(1) SPMD;
  - insurers referred to in Art. 13(1)-(6) of the Solvency II Directive;
  - AIFs, AIFMs, UCITS and UCITS management companies;
  - pension funds; and
  - public authorities.
- instruments covered by the definition of own funds within the meaning of CRR;
- debt securities (bonds) issued by a bank;
- deposits arising from transactions in connection with which there has been a criminal conviction for the offence of money laundering; and
- bank savings deposits in respect of home purchase loans, to the extent that these are set off to pursuant to related home acquisition debt under Art. 3:265d FSA (Art. 29.01(2) SPMD).

In the past, the CBb corrected DNB by ruling that subordinated deposits held at DSB Bank did not meet the definition of own funds within the meaning of the CRR and therefore fell within the scope of the DGS. This was the result of the CBb taking the view that it could not be determined that relevant deposit agreements did not contain any provisions in which, under certain circumstances, the deposits could be accelerated in any other way than by way of liquidation of DSB Bank (Court of Rotterdam, 29 July 2010).

The clients eligible for payment under the DGS are:

- persons who hold deposits on their own behalf and for their own account;
- persons who collectively hold a deposit with the bank; and
- third parties for the benefit of which a person holds an account in its own name but for the account of such third party pursuant to an agreement or legal provision (Art. 29.02 SPMD).

Annex a to the SPMD determines which deposits are not guaranteed. These include, for example, deposits from professional investors, professional market participants and major legal entities.

In the case a bank goes bankrupt, DNB publishes news about the DGS on its website and in the national press. Deposit holders can login to a special website. On this website they can determine the compensation to which they are entitled and indicate to which account the amount must be paid (Art. 29.04 and Art. 29.07 SPMD). DNB transfers the relevant amount within fifteen business days following the day on which DNB opens the DGS (Art. 29.08 and Art. 29.05(3) SPMD).

Compensation under the DGS is financed by a risk-based contribution that is collected 'ex ante' from the participating banks (the Deposit Guarantee Fund, see Arts. 29.11-29.13 SPMD). If the DGS proves to be insufficient, DNB will subsequently apportion the remaining costs to all participating banks that fall within the scope of the DGS (Art. 29.14 SPMD).

55 Investment principles and investment policies of PPIs

A PPI must draw up a statement of investment principles for each pension scheme that it operates, which is updated at least every three years (Art. 3:267a FSA). This statement includes at least the investment risk weighting methods applied for the assessment of investment risks, the risk management procedures and the strategic allocation of assets in the light of the nature and duration of the pension schemes and an explanation of environmental, corporate social responsibility and governance considerations. This statement must be amended immediately after any change to the investment principles (Art. 3:267a(2) FSA).

Additionally, a PPI must conduct an investment policy that is in accordance with the prudent person rule and is based in particular on the following principles (Art. 3:267b(1) FSA):

- the assets are invested solely in the interest of the pension participants and beneficiaries and in such a way that the security, quality, liquidity and return of the investments as a whole are guaranteed (Art. 3:267b(2) FSA);
- the assets are mainly invested in financial instruments which are admitted to trading on a regulated market, MTF or an equivalent system in a non-member State (Art. 3:267b(3) FSA); and
- a PPI does not enter into loans as a debtor, with the exception of loans taken out for liquidity purposes, and does not act as a guarantee for the benefit of third parties (Art. 3:267b(4) FSA).

These rules are further elaborated in the PRD (see Art. 124 PRD).

For example:
No more than 5% of the portfolio is allowed to be invested in the contributing company for the particular scheme. The investments are valued at market value.

The investment policy of a PPI that is governed by the social and labour law of a non-member state does not have to comply with the above (Art. 3:267b FSA and Art. 123 PRD).

If the PPI does not meet the minimum capital requirements, the solvency requirements or if it does not comply with the investment restrictions or the aforementioned prohibition on granting loans and guarantees, DNB may:

- limit the PPI's power of disposition over its assets; or
- prohibit the PPI to dispose over its assets without DNB's authorization thereto (Art. 3:267c FSA).

The PPI may invoke the invalidity of a legal act performed in violation of the restriction imposed by DNB against its counterparty if the latter was or should have been aware of the measure (Art. 3:267c(4) FSA). As soon as the PPI meets the requirements again, DNB must disapply the restriction (Art. 3:267c(5) FSA).

56 Consolidated supervision of financial firms

The FSA includes additional provisions for groups of companies of which one or more financial firms are a part, the so-called consolidated supervision.

Consolidated supervision means that supervision is based on the consolidated financial position of a financial firm that is part of a group.

Different types

For a good understanding of supervision at group level, it is important to note that:

- groups are subject to consolidated supervision if either the group parent company is a financial firm or the activities of the group focus solely or mainly on the financial sector. This supervision is exercised over financial conglomerates, (groups of) financial holding companies and insurance directive groups (all defined in Art. 1 FSA); and
- groups are supervised of which the parent company is not a financial firm and in which only one subsidiary is a financial firm, but which firm plays only a (relatively) minor role within the group. The parent undertaking of such a group is a mixed-activity holding company. Groups of mixed-activity holding companies are not subject to consolidated supervision (which is the case for financial conglomerates, financial holding company groups and insurance directive groups). However, intra-group transactions must be reported (Art. 3:280 FSA).

Additionally, it is important to distinguish between group supervision on financial conglomerates, financial holding groups and insurance directive groups:

- financial conglomerates are groups of which the parent company may or may not be a financial firm and whose subsidiaries are a combination of banks, investment firms and insurers. Therefore, the supervision on financial conglomerates concerns supervision of groups that conduct banking, investment and

insurance activities and follows from the Financial Conglomerates Directive; and
- financial holding company groups and insurance directive groups are also referred to as 'banking groups' or 'insurance groups'.

Examples are:
- **Banking groups**: these consist of banks, investment firms and payment institutions, such as ABN AMRO group;
- **Insurance groups**: these consist of different (types of) insurers , such as the Univé group; and
- **Financial conglomerates**: these consist of both insurers and banks or investment firms, such as the Aegon group.

The rules on consolidated supervision of banking groups and insurance groups are of a prudential and complementary nature. The rules on consolidated supervision apply in addition to the rules that are applicable to financial firms on an individual level. In certain cases, the consolidated supervision may replace part of the prudential supervision on an individual level on an individual financial firm.

Supervision of financial conglomerates is developed to complement the consolidated supervision of banking groups and insurance groups.

Regulator

Furthermore, the distinction between competent regulators is important. If the relevant legislation that applies to the relevant group (financial conglomerate, banking group or insurance group) stipulates that the Dutch regulator is competent, then this regulator is DNB, unless the ECB is the competent regulator pursuant to Art. 4 or 6 of the SSM Regulation.

Exemption

DNB has the option not to subject a firm that is part of an insurance group or financial conglomerate to consolidated supervision if:

- the firm is seated in a non-member state in which there are constitutional impediments to the provision of the information that is necessary in order to supervise the relevant firm;
- the firm to be subjected to such supervision is considered to be of negligible importance in the light of the objectives of such supervision, unless several firms belonging to the same group that may be excluded on an individual level are together not considered to be of negligible importance; or
- taking into account the financial position of such firm would be misplaced or misleading in the light of the objectives of such supervision (Arts. 3:270 and 3:296(5) FSA).

DNB and (in the case of a group with a significant bank) the ECB have the same option in relation to a firm that is part of a banking group (Art. 19 CRR).

Banking groups

The regulator that is responsible (the group regulator) is designated on the basis of Arts. 111(1)-111(4) CRD (Art. 3:275 FSA). In short, the following regulators qualify for designation as the competent regulator:

- in the case of a licensed parent bank seated in the EEA that is the head of a financial conglomerate: the national regulator of the member state of that conglomerate is competent;

- if the parent company is a licensed bank seated in the EEA, or if it is the head of a financial conglomerate, and to banks in more than one member state are granted a license: the national regulator that is competent to supervise the bank in that member state in which the parent company is established;
- where multiple parent companies can be identified that are banks with a banking license in the EEA or are the parent of a financial conglomerate, and a licence is granted to multiple banks in more than one member state: the national competent authority of the member state in which the bank with the highest balance sheet value is seated; or
- if the parent company is a licensed bank in the EEA or is the parent of a financial conglomerate, and a licence is granted to multiple banks in more than one member state, but not in the member state in which the parent company is established: the national regulator of the member state in which the bank with the highest balance sheet value is seated.

In case a Dutch bank or investment firm is a subsidiary of another licensed bank in the EEA, the regulator of the other member state will be the regulator. Under certain circumstances, DNB can consent to another regulator exercising the consolidated supervision (Art. 111(5) CRD).

Under certain circumstances, DNB or the ECB may also qualify as the competent regulator for consolidated supervision in case of a Dutch bank or investment firm with a parent undertaking established in a non-member state (Art. 3:277 FSA).

Elements of supervision

The supervision of banking groups relates to (Art. 3:276 FSA):

- the organisation of the group's business operations, which must be integer and controlled (Art. 3:17(1) and (2)(c) FSA);
- the solvency within the group (Art. 3:57 FSA);
- the capital buffer within the group (Art. 3:62a FSA);
- the acquisition of participations in certain firms (Art. 3:96(1)(b) FSA); and
- intra-group positions and agreements (Art. 3:280(2) FSA and Part 4 CRR).

Insurance groups

The regulator that is competent (the group supervisor) is designated in accordance with Art. 247 of the Solvency II Directive. In short, the following supervisors are eligible for designation as the competent regulator:

- if the parent of the group is a licensed (re)insurer: the national regulator of the member state in which that (re)insurer is seated; or
- if the parent of the group is not a licensed (re)insurer:
  - the national regulator of the member state in which one of subsidiaries, being licensed (re)insurers, are being granted its licence;
  - the national regulator of the member state in which the subsidiary with the highest balance sheet value is seated.

In particular cases and at the request of one of the other national regulators, the relevant national regulators may jointly decide to deviate from the criteria for the designation of the responsible regulator if the application of these criteria would be inappropriate, taking into account the structure of the group and the relative importance of the (re)insurers' activities in the different member states, and may jointly designate another national regulator as the competent group regulator.

Additionally, there is a committee of supervisors composed (mainly) of the group regulators and the national regulators of the licensed insurers in the insurance group.

Elements of supervision

Group supervision of insurance directive groups relates to:

- **Solvency**: the parent of the insurance directive group must ensure compliance with the solvency requirement, which must be calculated in accordance with the standard method in the Solvency II Directive (Art. 3:288a FSA). The parent of the insurance directive group must publish a report on the solvency and financial condition of the group on an annual basis (Art. 3:288i FSA);
- **ORSA** (Own-Risk and Solvency Assessment): an insurance group must conduct an assessment of its own risk and solvency at group-level (Art. 3:288h(4) FSA); and
- **Reporting obligations**: the parent of an insurance group must report all significant risk concentrations and significant intra-group positions and agreements to DNB (Art. 3:288e and Art. 3:288f FSA).

Financial conglomerates

This regime applies if the banking and investment activities as well as the insurance activities constitute a minimum of 10% of the balance sheet total of the group or if the smallest fraction exceeds EUR 6 billion (Art. 3:290 FSA).

The regulator responsible for supervision of financial conglomerate (the coordinator) is designated on the basis of Art. 10 of the Financial Conglomerates Directive. The following regulators are eligible for designation as the responsible regulators:

- if the parent of the group is a regulated entity: the national regulator of the member state in which the parent company is established; or
- if the parent of the group is not a regulated entity: the national regulator of the member state in which the regulated subsidiary with the largest balance sheet value is seated; or
- if Art. 4(1)(h) of the SSM Regulation applies: the ECB.

Elements of supervision

Group supervision of financial conglomerates relates to:

- reporting on significant risk concentrations (Art. 3:297 FSA);
- solvency requirements (Art. 3:296 FSA);
- reporting on intra-group agreements and positions (Art. 3:298 FSA); and
- reporting on the organisation of business operations and the firm structure (Art. 3:299 FSA).

V Part on Special measures and provisions concerning financial firms (Part 3A)

57 *General information*

There is a framework of rules for the recovery and resolution of banks and investment firms (of a certain size) that are in, or are at risk of getting into, financial difficulties. This is provided for in Section 3A.1 and concerns the implementation of the Recovery and Resolution of Banks and Investment Firms Directive (**BRRD**).

A similar framework exists outside the FSA for significant banks (and their group companies) within the Member States participating in the SSM (the eurozone). This is provided for in the Regulation on single resolution mechanism Regulation (Regulation (EU) No 806/2014, **SRMR**).

For the recovery and resolution of insurers there is a similar regime in Chapter 3A.2. This is based on the framework for banks and investment firms as mentioned above, but is less comprehensive. Therefore, the recovery and resolution regime as described below is also broadly applicable to insurers, with the exception of:

- the contractual resolvability clause;
- the minimum requirement for own funds and eligible liabilities (**MREL**);
- the early intervention phase; and
- the write-down or conversion of capital instruments (**WDCCI**).

Scope

The following entities having their seat in the Netherlands are within the scope of these resolution measures:

- banks;
- investment firms subject to the minimum capital requirement of € 730,000;
- certain holdings of groups with one of the abovementioned financial firms in the group, and their subsidiaries that are financial institutions (Art. 3A:2 FSA);
- insurers subject to supervision of DNB;
- certain (insurance) holdings of a group; and
- Dutch branches of insurers having their head office in a non-Member State (Art. 3A:78 FSA).

A group of these 'entities' that are jointly subject to consolidated supervision (see No 56) is also referred to as a 'consolidation group' for the purposes of this regime.

Furthermore, these resolution measures apply – irrespective of the applicable law – to the assets and liabilities of the relevant entity, to financial instruments issued by or with the assistance of that entity and to agreements entered into by the entity (Art. 3A:3 FSA).

Powers

The so-called 'resolution authority' (in the Netherlands; DNB) is charged with certain powers and obligations for the next three successive stages:

- the preparation phase (see No 58);
- the early intervention phase (see No 59); and
- the resolution phase (see No 60).

58 *The preparation phase*

Resolutionplan

The preparation phase consists of recovery planning and resolution planning. The former consists of the obligation for banks and investment firms to draw up their own recovery plans pursuant to Art. 3:17(2)(c) FSA (see No 44). For insurers, this obligation consists of drawing up a preparatory crisis plan pursuant to Art. 3:288i1 FSA.

DNB is responsible for establishing a resolution plan for investment firms that do not belong to a consolidation group and for consolidation groups that are not subject to the SRMR of which DNB is the group resolution authority (Art. 3A:9 FSA). In doing so, DNB must:

- determine the extent to which the entity or group concerned is resolvable; and
- on the basis of that assessment, identify any substantial impediments to the resolvability and, if necessary, impose measures on the entity or group to which that entity belongs in order to reduce or remove these impediments (Arts. 3A:10 FSA and 3A:11 FSA).

The substantive requirements of the SRMR apply *mutatis mutandis* to the resolution plan (Arts. 3A:9(4) FSA, 3A:10 FSA and 3A:11(3) FSA in conjunction with Art. 8 SRMR, Art. 10(1)-(6) SRMR and Art. 10(10) SRMR (and Art. 17 BRRD)).

If the resolution board or DNB considers that the proposed measures will not remove or reduce sufficiently the impediments to resolvability, DNB has the power to impose measures on the entity or group, including a requirement that the entity:

- limits exposures;
- divests specific assets;
- limits or suspends specific activities;
- changes the legal or operational structures;
- sets up a financial (EU) parent holding company; or
- issues eligible liabilities (Art. 3A:11a, in conjunction with Art. 10(11) SRMR).

Contractual resolvability clause

The entities subject to this regime must include in their agreements governed by the law of a third country, which contain obligations that would qualify for application of the WDCCI and bail-in powers of DNB (see No 60), a provision in which the counterparty agrees to the possible application of these powers and the consequences thereof (Art. 3A:13 FSA). This is in order to prevent the other party from being able to rely on the fact that these powers are not recognised by the applicable law.

MREL

In addition, for investment firms and for the EU parent companies of a consolidation group, minimum requirement for equity and eligible liabilities (MREL) determined by DNB apply. This is the minimum bail-in buffer that must be maintained. For other entities within the consolidation group DNB may impose an MREL (Art. 3A:16 FSA). A connection with the SRMR is made here as well (see Art. 3A:14(2) FSA, 3A:15(2) FSA and 3A:16(2) FSA in conjunction with Art. 12 SRMR).

59 *The early intervention phase*

Binding instruction

During the early intervention phase, when the financial position of a bank, investment firm or EU parent holding company deteriorates, DNB (or the ECB) may, among other things, issue the following binding instructions requiring the management of the bank or investment firm as referred to in Art. 3A:2 FSA:

- to draw up an action plan (Art. 1:75(3) FSA in conjunction with Art. 27(1)(b) BRRD);
- to be replaced or removed (Art. 1:75(3) FSA in conjunction with Art. 27(1)(d) BRRD); and
- to execute the recovery plan (Art. 1:75(3) FSA in conjunction with Art. 27(1)(a) BRRD).

Shareholder approval

DNB (or the ECB) may also prescribe in certain circumstances that the board of the bank or investment firm as referred to in Art. 3A:2 FSA convenes a general meeting of shareholders, or convenes it itself, to approve certain resolutions (Art. 1:75a FSA in conjunction with Art. 27(1), preamble BRRD).

Appointment of a special administrator

DNB (or the ECB) may also appoint one or more special administrators to replace the management of the bank or investment firm as referred to in Art. 3A:2 FSA, if:

- the aforementioned instruction is insufficient;
- the appointment of an administrator (in accordance with Art. 1:76 FSA, see No 16) is insufficient; and
- there is:
  - a significantly deteriorated financial situation;

- an offence classified in the third penalty category under Art. 1:81(2) FSA; or
- a serious violation of the articles of association of the bank or investment firm as referred to in Art. 3A:2 FSA (Art. 1:76a(1) FSA).

The decision to appoint the special administrator must clearly set out:

- what role, duties and powers are assigned to the special administrator; and
- the rules concerning the consultation of the administrator or obtaining its approval, which the day-to-day policymakers must comply with before taking certain decisions or measures (Art. 1:76a(2) FSA).

Restriction of rights of counterparties during the early intervention phase

If the aforementioned measures have been taken or if a related event occurs, the counterparties of the bank or investment firm as referred to in Art. 3A:2 FSA are not allowed to:

- enforce security or appropriate collateral (under a financial collateral arrangement);
- exercise termination, netting or set-off rights;
- exercise rights of recovery on the assets of the bank or investment firm as referred to in Art. 3A:2 FSA; or
- exercise suspension rights or compromise the rights of the bank or investment firm as referred to in Art. 3A:2 FSA under the relevant agreement in any other way,

provided that the bank or investment firm as referred to in Art. 3A:2 FSA continues to fulfil its key obligations under the relevant agreement, which includes the provision of collateral (Art. 1:76b(1) FSA).

Zero-hour rule

The measures taken by the regulator have retroactive effect to 00.00 hours on the day on which the relevant measure is taken. This means that, from that moment on, a counterparty will be restricted in the exercise of its rights in the manner described above, unless it concerns:

- an obligation which has led to a transfer order already entered into a system (within the meaning of Art. 212a Bankruptcy Act (**BA**));
- an order for set-off in a system (or a payment, delivery or other legal act arising from this); or
- rights and obligations of the bank or investment firm as referred to in Art. 3A:2 FSA that are a result of its participation in the system (Art. 1:76b(4) FSA).

60 *The resolution phase*

First: write-down or conversion of capital instruments (WDCCI)

Before the resolution authority may use the resolution tools, it will first need to assess whether the capital deficit of the entity concerned can be addressed by means of the 'write-down or conversion of capital instruments' (Art. 3A:17(1) FSA).

When applying the WDCCI instrument, the following order applies (Arts. 3A:21 FSA-3A:25 FSA):

- Common Equity Tier 1 instruments (see No 46) are first reduced in proportion to the losses and the total amount thereof;
- the principal amount of the additional Tier 1 instruments (see No 46) is then written down or converted into Common Equity Tier 1 instruments, or both; and
- the principal amount of the Tier 2 instruments (see No 46) is written down or converted into Common Equity Tier 1 instruments, or both.

Only then: resolution

If the WDCCI is not sufficient to make the entity in question viable, the resolution authority will proceed with resolution (Art. 3A:18(1) FSA).

Conditions for resolution

Before resolution can take place, the following conditions must be met:

- the entity concerned fails or is likely to fail;
- there is no reasonable prospect that a private solution or the use of the regular supervisory instruments will improve the situation; and
- the resolution of the entity concerned is in the public interest (Art. 3A:18(1) in conjunction with Art. 18(1) SRMR).

An entity is deemed to have failed, or to be likely to fail, in any of the following circumstances:

- *the entity concerned no longer meets the conditions under which it was granted a licence or will not meet these conditions under in the foreseeable future;*
- *the assets of the entity concerned are worth less than or will be worth less than its liabilities in the foreseeable future;*

- *the entity concerned is unable, or will be unable in the foreseeable future, to pay its debts; or*
- *the entity in question needs (certain forms of) state aid in order to survive.*

The latter condition is fulfilled if the intervention is necessary and proportional and if standard insolvency proceedings would not lead to the same results.

Resolution principles

In exercising its powers, the resolution authority must comply, *inter alia*, with the following resolution principles:

- shareholders and holders of other core capital instruments of the entity under resolution bear the initial losses;
- creditors of the entity under resolution bear the losses after shareholders and holders of other core capital instruments;
- the management body and senior management of the entity under resolution are replaced;
- the management body and senior management of the entity under resolution shall provide any support necessary to accomplish the resolution objectives;
- natural persons and legal entities shall be held liable under civil or criminal law in accordance with national law for the failure of the entity;
- unless the BRRD states otherwise, creditors from the same category are treated equally;
- no creditor suffers greater losses than he would have suffered if an entity would have become insolvent under standard insolvency proceedings;
- guaranteed deposits are fully protected; and
- resolution measures shall be taken in accordance with the safeguards laid down in the BRRD (Art. 1a Regulation on the

exercise of duties and cross-border cooperation of financial regulators FSA in conjunction with Art. 34(1) BRRD).

Resolution tools

The resolution tools are the following:

- sale of business (Section 3A.1.5.1 FSA);
- bridge institution (Section 3A.1.5.2 FSA);
- asset separation (Section 3A.1.5.3 FSA); and
- bail-in (Section 3A.1.5.4 FSA).

Transfer of business to a private party

In the case of the sale of business tool, the resolution authority decides on the transfer of:

- shares issued by the entity under resolution; or
- (part of) the assets and liabilities of the entity under resolution,

to another private party, who must pay a commercial price for it (Arts. 3A:28 FSA-3A:36 FSA).

Transition from an undertaking to a bridge institution

The bridge institution tool also covers the transfer of shares or assets, but to a bridge institution established to temporarily hold assets and liabilities, deposits or shares in order to maintain the critical functions of the entity under resolution (Arts. 3A:37 FSA to 3A:40 FSA).

Critical functions are activities and services which are essential for the functioning of the real economy or which, if discontinued, would be likely to lead to a disturbance of financial stability. Such a disturbance of financial stability could occur, for example, because of the interconnectedness, size or complexity of the institution or the irreplaceability of the services provided.

As regards a partial transfer of assets and liabilities in the event of a transfer of undertaking or use of the bridge institution, there are still some safeguards for the counterparties of the entity under resolution whose rights could be affected by such a transfer. The rights of those counterparties under:

- financial collateral arrangements, registered covered bonds, structured finance arrangements; and
- netting agreements, set-off agreements and security arrangements,

will not be affected by a partial transfer of business (Art. 3A:60 FSA).

In addition, these measures leave transfer orders in systems (within the meaning of Art. 212a BA) intact, is so far as these measures would affect the functioning of that system, *e.g.* because the measures would lead to the withdrawal of the transfer order (Art. 3A:59(2) FSA).

Asset separation

When applying the asset separation tool, the resolution authority decides that assets (and liabilities other than issued shares) are transferred to an asset and liability management entity. This tool is used to split off the 'bad parts' of the entity under resolution (the 'bad bank') and maintain the healthy parts. This instrument may only be used in combination with other resolution instruments in order to prevent the entity under resolution from gaining an unfair competitive advantage (Art. 3A:41(2) FSA).

Bail-in

The bail-in instrument (Section 3A.1.5.4 FSA) mainly concerns the conversion of liabilities into entitlements to newly issued core capital instruments or other property instruments to ensure the costs of the resolution of the entity in resolution are limited as much as possible for the taxpayer. With the bail-in tool these costs will be borne by the shareholders, holders of other core capital instruments and creditors of the failing institution.

61 Special measures

In addition to the aforementioned resolution tools, the resolution authority may take a number of special measures if deemed appropriate by the resolution authority (Section 3A.1.5.5 FSA).

Measures within the context of the corporate structure
DNB may, for example, appoint a special director and restrict the rights of other corporate bodies of the entity under resolution.

For example:
The exercise of voting rights by the shareholder of the entity (Art. 3A:49 FSA).

Also, DNB can convert the legal form of the entity concerned if necessary for the write-down and conversion of capital instruments, including when exercising the bail-in tool (Art. 3A:50 FSA).

Restriction of rights of counterparties during the resolution phase
In relation to an agreement to which the entity under resolution is a party, DNB may decide to:

- terminate or amend that agreement (Art. 3A:51 FSA);
- suspend the payment and delivery obligations of the entity under resolution under that agreement (Art. 3A:52 FSA); or

- limit and suspend the rights and powers of those counterparties, including their termination rights and rights of recourse (Arts. 3A:53 FSA and 3A:54 FSA).

These restrictions or suspensions may not be considered as a default under the relevant agreement (Art. 3A:55 FSA).

In addition, the restrictions under Art. 1:76b FSA (cf. No 59) also apply to all measures that can be taken under the resolution regime of Part 3A (Art. 3A:57 FSA).

Zero-hour rule

The special measures referred to above have retroactive effect to 00.00 hours on the day on which the relevant measure was taken, unless, in so far as is relevant, it concerns:

- an obligation which has led to a transfer order already entered into a system (within the meaning of Art. 212a BA);
- an order for set-off in a system (or a payment, delivery or other legal act arising from this); or
- a payment or delivery obligation guaranteed by the deposit guarantee scheme or investor compensation scheme (Arts. 3A:52(4) FSA, 3A:53(2) FSA and 3A:54(3) FSA).

Trade in financial instruments

Finally, DNB can request the AFM to exercise its powers under Arts. 1:77d FSA and 1:77e FSA in order to suspend or interrupt trading in financial instruments issued by the entity under resolution or to exclude those financial instruments from trading (Art. 3A:56 FSA).

62 Legal protection

As regards the legal protection against these resolution measures, the rules do not deviate from the general rules in the FSA in combination with the GALA. However, the legal protection has been further specified on a number of points. For example, the time limit for appealing to a decision to apply the WDCCI instrument is ten days (Art. 3A:64(1) FSA). In addition, an appeal against a decision under Part 3A of the FSA, contrary to Art. 6:6 GALA, is only inadmissible if the requirement of Art. 6:5(1)(d) GALA is not met (Art. 3A:64(2) FSA). Furthermore, there is no possibility for a *pro forma* appeal (Art. 3A:64(3) FSA).

The administrative judge must deal with each case within the framework of Part 3A in accordance with Art. 8:52 GALA in an accelerated manner and must render a decision within fourteen days after receipt of the notice of appeal (Art. 3A:64(6) FSA).

VI Part on Conduct of business supervision of financial firms (Part 4)

63 Introduction

Scope

The conduct of business rules for financial firms are included in Part 4. They apply to:

- managers of Dutch AIFs, the AIFs themselves and their depositaries;
- UCITS management companies, the UCITS themselves and their depositaries;
- investment firms with their seat in the Netherlands or in a third country;
- clearing institutions, when acting for clients with their seat in the Netherlands;
- financial service providers;
- financial institutions with their seat in the Netherlands and with a declaration of supervised status, which are permitted to perform activities pursuant to Chapter 2.2;
- payment service providers;
- pension fund custodians; and
- data reporting service providers whom are permitted to provide data reporting services in the Netherlands pursuant to Section 2.2.12a (Art. 4:1(1) FSA).

As such, this goes beyond just licensed entities. Also, parties that are excluded from the licence obligation and foreign passport holders are in scope. Investment firms with their seat in a member state (other than the Netherlands) are only (partially) subject to the Dutch conduct of business rules when they operate from a branch in the Netherlands (Art. 4:1(2) FSA).

Investment banks: banks that (also) provide investment services or perform investment activities are also referred to as 'investment banks'. It is important to note that the additional conduct of business rules discussed in this chapter for the provision of investment services also apply to them.

The conduct of business rules do not apply to:

- foreign AIFMs of which the Netherlands is the host member state who:
  - through the provision of services; or
  - from a branch in the Netherlands (except for Arts. 4:9, 4:10 and 4:37e FSA),
  - are managing Dutch AIFs or who are offering units in AIFs in the Netherlands; and
- 'light' managers (see No 31), except for Art. 4:37p FSA (Art. 4:1(3-6) FSA).

Types of conduct of business rules

The conduct of business rules can be distinguished into:

- general conduct of business rules that apply to all financial firms falling within the scope (Section 4.1.1 FSA to 4.2.4A FSA) (see No 64- 69); and
- additional conduct of business rules that only apply to a specific financial firm or to a specific financial service (Section 4.3.1 FSA to 4.3.8 FSA) (see No 70-78).

Each provision must be carefully examined to identify to which financial firm it applies. For example, Art. 4:9(2) FSA is only addressed to financial service providers. In addition, an exception to some general conduct of business rules apply to certain financial firms (Arts. 4:8 FSA, 4:12 FSA and 4:18 FSA). Hereinafter, for the sake of convenience, we will refer to financial firms and we will also not refer to data reporting service providers separately.

64 Suitability

The day-to-day policy must be determined by persons who are qualified with respect to a financial firm's ordinary course of business (Art. 4:9(1) FSA). In addition, members of a supervisory body (*e.g.* a supervisory board), if any, must be qualified for carrying out this supervision.

Who should be considered persons in charge of day-to-day policy is only specified in the explanatory notes to the application forms, the so-called 'fill-in instruction' of the AFM.

It concerns (according to the AFM):

- persons who formally hold the position of director within the undertaking (statutory directors); and
- persons who do not formally hold the position of statutory director within the undertaking but who are, de facto, in charge of the undertaking.

If persons can exercise actual substantial influence on the day-to-day policy or decision-making process regarding the long-term strategy of the undertaking, they should also be considered as day-to-day policymakers.

This may follow from the articles of association, regulations, (shareholder) agreements, internal agreements or factual circumstances (see Parliamentary History II 2005/06, 29708, No 20).

Assessment

The Policy Rule Suitability 2012 provides further detail on the eligibility requirement and states that suitability consists of:

- knowledge;
- skills; and
- professional behaviour.

In any event, this should be reflected in the education, work experience and competences of the policymaker and the ongoing application thereof. As such, the AFM or DNB assesses the suitability of a person based on his or her education, work experience and competences. This person must be suitable in relation to:

- governance, organisation and communication;
- products, services and markets in which the undertaking operates;
- controlled and sound business operations; and
- balanced and consistent decision-making.

The assessment will take into consideration:

- the role of the policymaker; and
- the type, size, complexity and risk profile of the undertaking.

Moreover, the regulator considers whether a person becomes part of a body. Therefore, it will look at the functioning of that body as a collective.

Suitability is tested:

- before a person takes a position, when applying for a licence or when there is the intention of a person to take a position; and
- after a person has taken a position, if there is reason to do so.

Oath or solemn affirmation

Finally, day-to-day policymakers and members of a supervisory board must take the oath as set out in the Regulation Oath or Solemn Affirmation for the Financial Sector 2015 within three months after commencing their activities (Art. 4:9(8) FSA).

In addition, also persons who:

- can materially influence the risk profile of financial firms; or
- within financial firms, are directly involved with the provision of financial services,

must take an oath or make a solemn affirmation (Art. 4:15a(1) FSA). The relevant financial firm must itself determine which employees fall within the scope of this requirement.

The purpose of taking the oath or making a solemn affirmation is to promote and maintain trust in the financial sector.

65 Knowledge and competence

Whereas the suitability rules apply to the higher echelon, the so-called 'client-facing employees' of a financial service provider are subject to the professional competence rules (Art. 4:9(2) FSA). This requirement is further set out in the MCSD (Arts. 5-11d MCSD).

Client-facing employees are employees who have substantive contact with clients. In any case this includes employees who advise clients on a financial product, such as: life insurances, non-life insurances, pensions and mortgage loans. Also, employees who inform a customer about, for example, the composition or functioning of a financial product are considered client-facing employees.

A financial service provider meets the knowledge and competence requirement if:

- its business operations sufficiently safeguard the competent provision of financial services to customers/clients;
- the client-facing employees who are advising clients, are in the possession of a recognised certificate; and
- these client-facing employees comply with the rules on permanent education (Art. 6 MCSD).

As to the certificates, there are nine professional qualifications:

- consumer credit (consumer);
- consumer credit (mortgage);
- non-life insurance (private);
- non-life insurance (business);
- health insurances;
- assets;
- income insurance;
- mortgage loan; and
- pension.

There are various modules under each qualification, varying from mbo to hbo+ level. Advisers must obtain a certificate for every qualification on which they advise from a recognised examination institute (Art. 7 and Art. 9 MCSD). The examination for the certificate must be retaken at least every three years.

The obligation to follow permanent education is an open standard. Therefore, the AFM has not specified any requirements with respect thereto, but has indicated that it considers it important:

- that the client-facing employee is permanently informed on the recent developments; and
- the client-facing employee can apply these recent developments in their day-to-day practice.

Thus, the client-facing employee must be aware of current developments and, for example, understand whether (an advice on) an existing product must be altered as a result of amended legislation and regulations.

The examination institutes are appointed by the Minister of Justice (Art. 11a MCSD). The Minister also maintains the central examination database in which the examinations are registered (Art. 11e MCSD).

In addition to the knowledge and competence rules for client-facing employees of a financial service provider, there are also knowledge and competence rules for certain persons working for investment firms. This concerns the persons who inform clients about financial instruments, investment services or ancillary services or who are directly involved in advising clients about financial instruments. These rules have been further set out in Art. 5a MCSD and the Regulation Knowledge and Competences of Investment Firm Employees FSA.

66 Trustworthiness

The trustworthiness (*i.e.* integrity) of:

- persons who determine the day-to-day policy of a financial undertaking or co-policymakers who partly determine the policy; and
- members of a supervisory body (*e.g.* a supervisory board),

must be beyond doubt (Art. 4:10 FSA).

Persons who are partly determining the policy are, according to the AFM's 'fill-in instruction', persons who can *'exercise significant influence on the day-to-day policy'* of the undertaking.

According to the AFM, co-policy makers are in any case:

- persons who have more than 50% of the shares or control in the undertaking; and
- persons who are factually in a position to influence the day-to-day policy of the undertaking substantially.

The provision has deliberately been formulated in such a way that it also includes persons who factually exercise substantial influence on policy or decision-making regarding the long-term strategy of the financial firm. This may follow from the articles of association, regulations, (shareholder) agreements, internal agreements or factual circumstances (e.g. certain veto rights) (*see* Parliamentary History II 2005/06, 29708, No 20).

Assessment

The trustworthiness requirement is further set out in Arts. 12-16 MCSD.

The reason for the trustworthiness test is that the integrity of persons and undertakings who are active in the financial markets are of great importance for the trust of the public in these markets and the undertakings active in these markets.

The AFM tests trustworthiness on the basis of the person's intentions, actions and antecedents. In any case, the trustworthiness is not considered beyond doubt if there are certain criminal, financial, supervisory or administrative antecedents (see Art. 15 MCSD in conjunction with appendix C to the MCSD).

For example:
When a person has been convicted of an offence listed in Section 1 of annex C less than eight years ago, the trustworthiness of that person is not considered beyond doubt.

The trustworthiness is tested:
- before a person takes a position, when applying for a licence or when there is the intention to take a position; and
- after a person has taken a position, if there is reason to do so.

67 Integrity policy

Financial firms must pursue an integrity policy conducive to ensuring the integrity of the undertaking's operations. This means that they should prevent:
- that it or its employees are involved in:
  - criminal offences;
  - other violations of the law; or
  - other acts contrary to a social norm; or

- that the actions of clients (*e.g. fraud or illegal practices such as money laundering*) may damage the trust in the financial firm or in the financial market as a whole; or
- conflicts of interest (*e.g. ancillary functions of directors with business relations, providing loans to directors and private investments*) (Art. 4:11 FSA).

With respect to financial service providers, only the first aspect applies, apart from the social norm (Art. 4:11(2) FSA).

To this end, an integrity policy should be drawn up based on the analysis of integrity risks relevant to the concerning financial firm.

Minimum requirements

This integrity policy is subject to minimum requirements. Those are:

- the policy must be laid down in procedures and measures; and
- the financial firm must:
  - ensure independent monitoring of the implementation of the policy, procedures and measures; and
  - have procedures in place to ensure that any identified defects or deficiencies in relation to the sound business operations of the business lead to appropriate adjustments (Art. 17 MCSD).

68 *Structuring and organisation*

Structure of control

Financial firms may not be connected in any formal or actual control structure to persons or legal entities:

- in such a way that it impedes, or may impede adequate supervision of the relevant financial firm; and
- if the law of a third country applies to those persons or legal entities, it impedes, or may impede adequate supervision of the concerning financial firm (Art. 4:13 FSA).

The background of this provision is to prevent the AFM from being frustrated in the performance of its supervisory duties.

Organisation of business operations

Financial firms must organise their business operations in such a way that it guarantees controlled and sound business operations (Art. 4:14 FSA).

Note: *this obligation is different from Art. 4:11 FSA, which relates to having a policy to guarantee controlled and sound business operations.*

The 'business operations' include the following aspects:

- general aspects (aspects of the business operations that do not relate to integrity, prudential or conduct of business aspects);
- integrity aspects;
- prudential aspects; and
- conduct of business aspects.

The general, prudential and conduct of business aspects relate to *controlled* business operations. The integrity aspects relate to *sound* business operations.

General aspects

Business processes and risks must be controlled (Art. 4:14(2)(a) FSA). 'Controlling' includes the entire process of establishing, managing, monitoring and adjusting objectives and processes.

- The business operations must provide for:
  - clear decision-making procedures and a clear, balanced and adequate organisational structure;
  - a clear, balanced and adequate division of tasks, powers and responsibilities;
  - unambiguous reporting lines;
  - an adequate system of information and communication facilities; and
  - adequate internal control procedures to ensure compliance with decisions and procedures at all levels (Art. 30(1) MCSD).
- The business operations must be tailored to the nature, size, risks and complexity of the financial firm and its activities (Art. 30(2) MCSD).
- In the case of UCITS management companies, there must be an organisational unit that independently assesses the effectiveness of the organisational structure (the 'audit function') at least once a year, with the task of:
  - establishing and implementing a control plan to examine and assess the adequacy and effectiveness of the financial undertaking's systems, internal control procedures and rules;
  - making recommendations based on the results thereof;
  - monitoring compliance with these recommendations; and
  - reporting annually to the persons responsible for the day-to-day policy of the financial firm and to (if there is one) the 'audit committee' (Arts. 30(6) and 31a MCSD).

- In the case of UCITS management companies, there must be an organisational unit which independently and effectively performs a compliance function, with the task:
  - to oversee compliance with legislation and internal rules drawn up by the UCITS management company itself;
  - to advise the persons responsible for the UCITS management companies' compliance with legislation and internal rules;
  - to monitor the adequacy and effectiveness of internal rules and procedures;
  - to assess the effectiveness of the procedures in place and measures taken to address identified deficiencies in compliance with legislation and internal rules; and
  - to report at least annually to the persons who determine the day-to-day policy of the UCITS management company and to the supervisory body, if any, which monitors compliance with legislation and internal rules. In addition, this annual report must state whether measures have been taken in the event of identified deficiencies (Art. 31c MCSD).

There is a focused ('principle based') approach. A financial firm should make its own analysis of the risks and organise its business operations accordingly.

For investment firms, there are similar rules laid down in the Delegated Regulation (EU) No 2017/565, Delegated Regulation on Organisational Requirements (see also Art. 31b MCSD).

Integrity aspects

Sound business operations must be ensured (Art. 4:14(2)(b) FSA). This means that the policy based on Art. 4:11 FSA must actually be anchored in the organisation. To this end, a financial firm must, among other things:

- make a well-founded assessment of the trustworthiness of persons it wishes to appoint to an integrity-sensitive position;
- ensure the assessment of the trustworthiness of those who, other than on the basis of the employment contract, perform activities in an integrity-sensitive position;
- protect the integrity of the undertaking by having procedures and measures in place with respect to the acceptance of investors/clients;
- have procedures and measures in place with respect to the identification of investors/clients and the verification thereof;
- have procedures and measures in place with respect to the analysis of investor data, also in relation to the products purchased by the investors/clients, and the detection of atypical transaction patterns;
- ensuring the documentation and recording with respect to the acceptance and risk classification of clients; and
- examine, at the request of the AFM, if there are certain persons or institutions in its records who, according to the Minister's judgment, could damage the integrity of the financial sector in connection with suspected terrorist or related activities (Arts. 19-22 and Arts. 25-27 MCSD).

Financial service providers must ensure that there is no doubt as to the trustworthiness of their client-facing (temporary) employees, de facto supervisors and secondees, to the extent information relating to the content of financial services is exchanged (Art. 28 MCSD). Furthermore, there must be procedures and measures regarding to the processing and administrative recording of incidents (an 'incident scheme').

An incident is an 'act or event that poses a serious threat to the integrity of the business of a financial undertaking' (Art. 1 MCSD).

A financial firm must act as follows in the event of an incident:

- take measures aimed at:
  - managing the risks incurred; and
  - the prevention of recurrence; and
- inform the AFM immediately about the incident (Arts. 19, 24 and 29 MCSD).

Behavioural aspects

There must be orderly and transparent financial market processes, clear relationships between market participants and careful treatment of clients and investors (Art. 4:14(2)(c) FSA).

Product governance: financial firms offering or manufacturing financial products and making them available on the market must have adequate procedures and measures in place to ensure that:

- the interests of the consumer, client or, if applicable, the beneficiary of the financial product, must be taken into account in a balanced manner during the development of the financial product; and
- the financial product must demonstrably be the result of this balancing of interests (Art. 32(1) MCSD).

'Manufacturing' is usually done by intermediaries who manufacture a new product from existing products and advise or intermediate. For example, a situation in which the intermediary composes a product from two or more financial products and makes this product available on the market. These include, for example, intermediaries who combine a mortgage loan with a financial product that serves to repay that loan, such as life insurance, and

present it as a product. A product may also be manufactured by a party other than the supplier or intermediary who makes the product available on the market.

The procedures and measures must be laid down in a 'product governance process' and must in any case ensure that:

- the target market of the financial product is determined, by which it is analysed and described what the intended objective of the target market is;
- analyses are carried out in which the functioning of the product as a whole and its individual components are identified in different scenarios and show that, given the nature of the product, the financial product does not detract from its original objective;
- the product information and, to the extent as reasonably expected, the distribution of the financial product is adapted to the target market; and
- there will be frequent monitoring and, if necessary, an adjustment of the procedures and measures. The procedures or measures must demonstrably provide for the development of products that are in the interests of the consumer, client or beneficiary (Art. 32(2) MCSD).

AIFMs, UCITS management companies who are exclusively offer units to professional investors and financial service providers who offer or manufacture insurances against large risks and make it available on the market, are exempted from these rules (Art. 32(8) MCSD).

The product governance rules also apply to investment firms who issue, manufacture or assemble financial instruments and make them available on the market (Art. 32(6) MCSD). In addition, such investment firms must inform other investment firms providing investment services in respect of that financial instrument about the characteristics and risks of that financial instrument, the characteristics and objectives of the target market and the distribution strategy (Art. 32a MCSD and Art. 9 Delegated Implementing Directive MiFID2 (2017/593/EU)).

Furthermore, there are rules for investment firms distributing financial instruments. Those investment firms must have adequate procedures and measures in place to ensure that the financial instruments meet the needs, characteristics and objectives of the target market and that the distribution strategy is appropriate for the concerning target market. Further details can be found in Art. 32b MCSD.

Recording given advice: financial service providers advising a consumer or client on financial products must keep the information obtained from the consumer or client about its financial position, knowledge, experience, objectives and risk appetite (the 'client profile'), and the details of the product sold or recommended to it, for a period of five years from the time the advice is given (Art. 32d MCSD). This enables them to reconstruct the advice and demonstrate that they have passed the suitability test (see No 64).

The client profile should be clear enough for the financial service provider to be able to use that information to demonstrate that the product sold or recommended suits the client. The 'information about the product sold or recommended' refers to the information that can be used to determine which financial product has been advised to the client.

If the client purchases a product from or via the financial service provider other than the one advised by the financial service, it must also be in a position, for five years following the advice, to demonstrate that the consumer has not followed the advice (Art. 32d(5) MCSD).

The same requirement applies to credit providers to demonstrate that they have complied with their 'know-your-customer' requirement to prevent excessive lending (Art. 33 MCSD) (see No 70).

Conflicts of interest: a UCITS management company has procedures and measures in place to prevent and manage conflicts of interest between itself and its clients or between its clients.

These procedures and measures are designed to ensure that relevant persons involved in different business activities, where there is a risk of a conflict of interest, will carry out these activities independently. The procedures and measures include rules regarding:

- the exchange of information between relevant persons engaged in various activities where there is a risk of a conflict of interest;
- the monitoring of the activities of relevant persons providing services to clients whose interests may conflict;
- independent remuneration;
- measures to prevent or reduce the risk of a person exercising influence over the manner in which another person performs its activities; and
- measures to prevent or control the simultaneous or consecutive involvement of a person in various activities which may cause conflicts of interest (Art. 35a MCSD).

If a conflict of interest nevertheless arises, the UCITS management company must inform its clients (Art. 35b MCSD). For investment firms there are similar rules set out in Chapter II Section 3 of the Delegated Regulation on Organisational Requirements.

Personal transactions: a UCITS management company or investment firm has procedures and measures in place relating to personal transactions of its employees. These procedures and measures are designed to ensure that if a relevant person is involved in the conduct of activities that may give rise to a conflict of interest or has access to 'inside information' or other confidential information about clients or transactions with or for clients (summarised):

- no personal transaction is carried out by that person; and
- the relevant person does not advise (or recommend to) another person to enter into a transaction which would not be allowed if it was a personal transaction carried out by him- or herself (Art. 35c MCSD and Art. 29 Delegated Regulation on Organisational Requirements).

Investment research: an investment firm must also have procedures and measures in place to prevent conflicts of interest that may arise from the performance, manufacturing and distribution of investment research (so-called analyst reports).

Financial analysts engaged in investment research face a wide range of potential conflicts that may impair the objectivity and independence of the research. They can be influenced by interests of the investment firm or certain groups of clients which may conflict with the interests of those for whom the research is intended.

The procedures and measures should ensure the objectivity and independence of investment research conducted by financial analysts (Arts. 36 and 37 Delegated Regulation on Organisational Requirements).

Financial service providers

Similar rules apply to financial service providers for business operations, albeit only with respect to the last two aspects: integrity and orderly and transparent financial market processes (Art. 4:15 FSA). They, therefore, do not need to have an audit and compliance function.

Outsourcing

Financial firms who outsource activities to a third party must ensure that the third party complies with the applicable conduct of business rules of Part 4 (Art. 4:16 FSA). Some activities may not be outsourced (*e.g.* Arts. 38(2) and 38g MCSD).

Outsourcing is the delegation of a task to a third party for the performance of certain activities which the financial firm would normally carry out itself.

Several important additional rules stipulate that:

- a financial firm may not outsource activities if this would impede adequate supervision of compliance with Part 4 (Art. 37 MCSD);
- an AIFM may not delegate the functions of portfolio management and risk management to the depositary and it may not outsource activities to such an extent that the AIFM itself becomes a letterbox company (Art. 37a MCSD and Art. 20 AIFMD);
- a UCITS management company, a payment institution or an electronic money institution must inform the regulator, in some

situations, that it is outsourcing tasks (Arts. 38a and 38i MCSD); and

- an investment firm must lay down the outsourcing arrangement in a written outsourcing agreement and ensure that:
  - the third party has the expertise, capacity, sufficient resources, an appropriate organisational structure and any licence as required by law to carry out the outsourced activities reliably and professionally;
  - the third party actually carries out the outsourced activities in compliance with the applicable laws and that it establishes methods for assessing the third party's performance and continuously reviews the services provided;
  - it adequately monitors the performance of the outsourced activities and adequately manages the associated risks;
  - it takes appropriate action if it appears that the third party is not carrying out the work efficiently and in compliance with applicable law;
  - it maintains the necessary expertise and resources to effectively supervise the outsourced activities and manage the risks;
  - the third party shall inform the investment firm of any developments likely to have a material effect on its ability to carry out the outsourced activity efficiently and in compliance with applicable law;
  - it may, if necessary, terminate the outsourcing agreement with immediate effect without any consequences for the continuity or the quality of services provided to clients;
  - the third party cooperates with its regulators with respect to the outsourced work;
  - it, its auditors and its regulators have effective access to the data relating to the outsourced activities and the regulators

can carry out or arrange for on-site investigations at the third party;
- the third party protects all confidential information on the investment firm and its clients;
- it and the third party have a contingency plan that provides for emergency management and periodic monitoring of back-up facilities whenever this is deemed necessary with respect to the outsourced tasks; and
- the continuity and quality of the outsourced activities are maintained even in the event of termination of the outsourcing arrangement by transferring these activities to another third party or performing them itself (Art. 31 Delegated Regulation on Organisational Requirements).

Complaints handling

As a final element of sound business operations, financial firms must (except for investment firms):

- have in place an internal complaints procedure ensuring prompt and careful handling of complaints; and
- be registered with the KiFID Financial Complaints Institute (Art. 4:17 FSA).

To ensure that all persons involved in the complaints handling are aware of the procedure to be followed, a description must be drawn up (Art. 40 MCSD). Several timelines must be safeguarded by this procedure (Art. 44 MCSD), so that complaints are dealt with within a reasonable period of time.

The receipt of the complaint must be confirmed, and the complainant must be informed within two weeks about the timeframe in which the complaint will be dealt with. The complainant may submit the complaint directly to KiFID six weeks after receipt of the confirmation of receipt or eight weeks after submission of the complaint (Art. 43 MCSD).

In the event of a total or partial rejection of the complaint, the financial undertaking shall inform the complainant of the possibility of submitting the complaint to KiFID (Art. 42 MCSD).

In addition, the financial undertaking must maintain an adequate administration of complaints, where, at least, the following should be recorded:

- the name and address of the complainant;
- the complaint, with the corresponding date of receipt;
- a description of the complaint; and
- a description of the way in which it has dealt with the complaint.

The financial firm must keep the data for one year after the complaint has been dealt with (Art. 41 MCSD).

Some slightly different rules apply to payment service providers (Arts. 43(6) and 43a MCSD). For investment firms, similar rules are included in Art. 26 Delegated Regulation on Organisational Requirements.

69 Duty of care

Section 4.2.3 FSA contains a number of rules relating to the duty of care financial firms should exert. The applicability of these rules varies from one type of financial firm to another and sometimes depends on the type of client.

Information

An important principle of the FSA is that buyers of financial products receive sufficient information about those products. The rules on the provision of information can be divided into rules about:

- mandatory pre-contractual information;
- non-mandatory pre-contractual information (advertising); and
- mandatory information to be provided during the term of the agreement.

The following general rules apply to all information provided:

- information concerning a financial product or financial service provided by the financial firm must not prejudice the information requirement under Part 4;

For example, a credit advertisement shall not include information on interest that is inconsistent with the information on interest that is required to be provided prior to the conclusion of the agreement pursuant to Art. 4:20 FSA.

- the information provided must be accurate, clear and not misleading; and

As regards clarity, the average consumer or client may be taken as a starting point. The complexity of the financial product or service will also play a role.

- the commercial purpose of the information provided must be recognisable as such (Art. 4:19 FSA).

Pre-contractual information

Thus, prior to the conclusion of an agreement with a consumer or client, certain mandatory information must be provided that is relevant for an adequate assessment of the service or product (Art.

4:20(1) FSA). Which information this exactly is, is set out in the MCSD per product or service (see Arts. 57-66b MCSD) and, in the case of insurance contracts, in Art. 4:22a FSA.

For example, an investment firm must prior to:
- the provision of an investment or ancillary service to a client provide information about the investment or ancillary service, financial instruments, proposed investment strategies, execution venues and all costs and associated charges (Art. 58 MCSD); and
- advising on financial instruments inform the client on whether:
  - the advice is provided on a dependent or independent basis;
  - the advice is based on a broad or more limited analysis of different types of financial instruments; and
  - the client receives a periodic assessment of the suitability of the advised financial instruments (Art. 58a(1) MCSD).

Investment firms are also subject to the rules set out in Chapter IIIA Section 1 Delegated Regulation on Organizational Requirements.

Advertising; risk indicator, warning text and essential information document

There are also extensive rules on non-mandatory pre-contractual information (advertising) (see Arts. 52-56 MCSD and Art. 44 Delegated Regulation on Organisational Requirements). When advertising complex products insofar as they are insurances with an investment component or packaged retail investment products, the most important financial risks must be presented by including a 'risk indicator' (Art. 52 MCSD).

A product is, among other things, 'complex' if it is composed from two or more financial products that include at least one financial product whose value is subject to developments on the financial markets (Art. 1 MCSD). An example of a complex product is an investment-linked insurance.

The FRSCFU sets out rules on the format of the risk indicator. There are different risk indicators depending on the type of financial product.

Figure 2 Risk indicator

If the information does not relate to complex products, the general advertising guidelines set out in Appendix 12 to Art. 7:3 FRSCFU may apply. On this basis thereof, investment firms should have the following text prominently displayed in advertisements expressing expectations about the future or referring to past performance:

'The value of your investment may fluctuate. Results achieved in the past are no guarantee for the future.'

In addition, there is an obligation to draw up a Key Information Document (KID) with respect complex products insofar as they are insurances with an investment component or packaged retail investment products. A KID provides information on returns, risks and costs in a clear format, no longer than three A4 pages. The PRIIPs Regulation sets requirements for the content of the KID (see also No 12).

Ongoing information obligations

Finally, information about significant changes in the information provided during the pre-contractual phase (Art. 4:20 (3) FSA), as well as certain reports (see Arts. 67-80.0a MCSD and Chapter III Section 1 Delegated Regulation on Organizational Requirements) must be provided timely during the term of the agreement.

For example, a provider of mortgage loans with a floating interest rate must inform the consumer on paper, or by way of another sustainable source, prior to any change in the interest rate. In addition, it should also inform the consumer about:

- the adjusted annual cost percentage;
- the component or components which caused the change of the interest rate;
- the instalments due after the new interest rate has become applicable; and
- where applicable, changes in the number or frequency of the instalments (Art. 68a MCSD).

General duty of care

There is also a general duty of care for financial service providers, which means that a financial service provider must '*carefully observe the legitimate expectations of the consumer or beneficiary*' (Art. 4:24a(1) FSA). When giving advice, the financial service provider may only act in the interest of the consumer (Art. 4:24a(2) FSA). A similar requirement applies to the provision of investment services (Art. 4:90 FSA).

The legislator introduced the general duty of care for financial service providers because a service provider is deemed to have more knowledge and information than a consumer. The general duty of care should ensure that the financial service provider verifies that its acts or omissions do not adversely affect the interests of consumers.

The AFM can intervene in the event of a breach of the duty of care by issuing an instruction (and, if this is not complied with, possibly a fine or an order subject to a penalty), but only '*in the case of obvious wrongdoing that may damage the trust in the financial service provider or in the financial markets as a whole*' (Art. 4:24(2) FSA). In addition, a consumer may claim damages on the basis of the DCC (Art. 6:162 DCC).

Standard of care

A number of general standards of care apply to financial firms (Art. 4:25 FSA and Arts. 81-86ia MCSD). They relate to the following:

- **Cold calling**: investment firms are not allowed to approach clients on an unsolicited basis by using automatic calling systems without human intervention (Art. 81 MCSD). In addition, investment firms are not allowed to approach retail investors 'in person' to whom they have not yet provided investment services (Art. 82 MCSD).

- **Balance and margin monitoring requirement**: an investment firm may not execute transactions if the client's account balance is insufficient to meet the obligations arising from the transactions (Art. 85 MCSD). In addition, the investment firm must ensure that the client continuously has sufficient funds to meet its obligations where it has a position in financial instruments from which liabilities may arise (Art. 86 MCSD). If the funds are insufficient, the investment firm must ensure that the client provides collateral. If the client fails to do so, the investment firm must close the client's positions as soon as possible, but at the latest within five days.

For example:
If the client writes an option, the client may have a future obligation to buy or deliver shares.

- **Churning**: an investment firm must refrain from executing transactions on behalf of clients at such a frequency or of such a size that, considering the circumstances, this is evidently only intended for the benefit of the investment firm, except with respect to transactions for which the client has given instructions at its own initiative (Art. 84 MCSD). This prohibition prevents investment firms from executing unnecessarily large numbers of transactions to generate income from transactions costs.

70 *Client classification and know-your-customer*

Client classification

Investment firms are required to categorise their clients into one of the following categories (client classification):

- retail investors;
- professional investors (see No 9); and
- eligible counterparties (Art. 4:18a FSA).

Clients must be informed of this classification and it is possible for them to switch categories, per transaction or for the entire service relation (Arts. 4:18b-4:18d FSA and Art. 71(4) of the Delegated Regulation on Organisational Requirements). A request to be classified 'lower' is referred to as 'opt-down' and a request to be classified 'higher' is called 'opt-up'.

The category determines which conduct of business rules an investment firm must observe with respect to that client. For retail investors, the highest level of protection applies whereas for eligible counterparties the lowest level applies. For example, not all information obligations (Arts. 4:19, 4:20 and 4:22 FSA (see No 69)) apply when services are provided to professional investors, and a lighter know-your-customer test (only appropriateness instead of suitability (see below)). When dealing with eligible counterparties, those obligations (as well as the best execution obligation (see No 69)) do not apply at all (Art. 4:18b(1) FSA).

Know-your-customer

Before a financial firm provides services, it must first obtain the necessary information from the concerning client and establish a client profile. This is also referred to as the 'know-your-customer' assessment. Two different tests can be distinguished:

- a suitability test for investment advice and portfolio management (Art. 4:23 FSA); and
- an appropriateness test for other investment services (Art. 4:24 FSA).

For the suitability test, information should be obtained on:

- the financial position;
- knowledge;
- experience;
- objectives; and
- risk appetite,

of the client, to the extent relevant for investment advice and portfolio management.

This information is required to tailor the service to the obtained client profile. The extent to which information is collected will depend on the complexity of the product or service with respect to which advice is provided. Only the information that is reasonably relevant to that product or service should be obtained. More extensive information will have to be obtained where advice is provided on investments, whereas for simpler products less information about the consumer or client will be required.

For the appropriateness test, only information about knowledge and experience of the consumer or client needs to be obtained. If, on the basis of this information, it appears that the financial service is not suitable for the consumer or client, the client must be warned (Art. 4:24 (2) FSA). An exception to the appropriateness test applies to the provision of services that do not involve advice ('execution-only'), insofar:

- it concerns orders for certain 'simple' financial instruments, *e.g.* listed shares and units in UCITS (Art. 4:24(5)(a)-(f) FSA and Art. 80d MCSD);
- the service is provided on the initiative of the client (*reverse solicitation*);
- it does not also involve the provision of the ancillary service of 'granting credits or loans to an investor to allow him to carry out a transaction in one or more financial instruments, where the firm granting the credit or loan is involved in the transaction'; and
- the investment firm has informed the client in advance that it has not assessed the suitability of the service for the client (Art. 4:24(4) FSA).

For both tests, the information that is required to be obtained from the client depends on the outcome of the client classification and the entire service relation should be considered as to whether this is suitable and/or appropriate if additional financial services or products are offered.

Which information must be obtained from the client differs per type of client (Arts. 80a-80e MCSD). Schematically it looks like this:

Table 4 Appropriateness test

Test type	What services?	Required information (general)	What information for which type of client?
Suitability test (Art. 4:23 FSA)	- Investment advice - Portfolio management	- Financial situation - Knowledge - Experience - Investment objectives - Risk tolerance	- Eligible counterparties: N/A - Professional investors: – only in the case of investment advice: information on the financial situation not required – knowledge and experience is assumed to be present Retail investors: all information required
Appropriateness test (Art. 4:24(1) FSA).	All other investment services	- Knowledge - Experience	- Eligible counterparties: N/A - Professional investors: N/A - Retail investors: all information required

Furthermore, in the case of portfolio management services provided to a retail investor, the investment firm must periodically issue a suitability statement to the relevant investor (Art. 4:23(4) FSA).

71 Ban on inducements

There is a ban on inducements for financial service providers. This includes a prohibition to receive or pay inducements from the provider of a financial product for intermediating or advising with respect to that financial product (Art. 4:25a FSA and Art. 86c MCSD). Because of this ban, the financial link between providers and advisors or intermediaries is cut.

Inducement: a reward or fee, in any form whatsoever.

Scope

The ban on inducement applies to the following:

- payment protection insurance;
- complex products (see No 69);
- mortgage loans;
- life insurances;
- funeral expenses insurances;
- premium pension receivables;
- individual invalidity insurances; and
- other financial products to be designated by ministerial regulation (Art. 86c(1) MCSD).

As such, the ban on inducements does not apply to non-life insurances and to forms of consumer credit other than mortgage loans. However, these products are subject to rules on fee transparency (Art. 86d MCSD).

Exemptions

The ban on inducements does *not* apply to:

- inducements paid by the consumer/client, unless the amount of these commissions is evidently unreasonable in view of the nature and scope of the service;
- inducements necessary for providing the financial service, or making the financial service in question possible;
- inducements from one adviser/intermediary to another adviser/intermediary (provided that they are upstream in the chain examined by the client/consumer); and
- business gifts below € 100 on an annual basis (Art. 86c (2) MCSD).

Information obligation

For the provision of a financial service with respect to a financial product subject to the ban on inducements, the financial service provider must inform the consumer/client about, *inter alia*:

- the nature and scope of the service;
- the way in which the financial service provider is remunerated;
- the costs and charges of the service provided payable by the customer/client;
- the interests of the financial service provider which may be of influence on the services provided to the customer/client; and
- any other subjects which may be relevant to the adequate assessment of the provision of services by the consumer/client to be designated by lower regulation.

This information must be provided in a 'service-document' (Art. 86f MCSD). In addition, there is an obligation for a product provider to draw up a cost model. This cost model must be used to calculate the advice and distribution costs for concluding an agreement (Art. 86g MCSD).

In addition to this general ban on inducements, there is a similar ban on inducements for investment firms (Arts. 168a-168ac MCSD). However, unlike the inducement ban for financial service providers, the inducement ban for investment firms makes a distinction between the provision of services to professional and retail investors, with a lighter regime for the provision of services to professional investors.

72 Notification obligations

There are various reporting and notification obligations for financial firms to the AFM (Arts. 4:26-4:27a FSA and Arts. 87a-108 MCSD). The main obligation is to notify changes to previously provided information in the context of a licence application.

In addition, there is an obligation for auditors who audit the financial statements of financial firms to notify:

- any breach of applicable conduct of business rules in Part 4; and
- general circumstances leading to a refusal to provide an opinion on the truth and fairness of the financial statements (Art. 4:27 FSA).

73 *Offering investment objects*

A provider of investment objects must have a website and must have an investment object prospectus available (Art. 4:30a FSA). Extensive rules apply with respect to the content of this prospectus (Arts. 109 and 110 MCSD and Arts. 5:1-5:3 FRSCFU). This prospectus is different than the one the one required under the Prospectus Regulation when offering securities (see No 79). In addition, general information obligations apply. If the concerning investment objects qualifies as a packaged retail investment product or an insurance-based investment product with an investment component, a KID must be drawn up (see also No 69).

74 *Granting credit*

Mandatory participation in credit registration system

A credit provider is required to participate in a credit registration system (Art. 4:32 FSA). In the Netherlands, this is de Stichting Bureau Kredietregistratie (**BKR**). The BKR records any late payments when informed by the participants (such as banks, leasing companies, telecom providers, etc.).

If a credit provider decides not to grant credit to a consumer after consulting the BKR register, he must inform the consumer about:

- the outcome of the consultation with the BKR; and
- details of specific late payments.

In practice, this means that the credit provider will send a letter to the consumer stating that it will not grant him credit because of a registration with the BKR. Consumers can then contact the BKR for an explanation of the registration. If the credit provider does grant credit to the consumer, there is of course no need to provide information about the BKR consultation.

Pre-contractual information

Prior to the conclusion of a credit agreement with a consumer, certain mandatory information must be provided which is relevant for an adequate assessment of the credit (Art. 4:33 FSA). Which information this entails, is set out in the MCSD (Arts. 112-112e MCSD).

Creditworthiness test

A credit provider must carry out a 'creditworthiness test' on a consumer before concluding the credit agreement or if the amount of credit, or the credit limit, is increased (Art. 4:34 FSA). To this end, the credit provider:

- must obtain information on the financial position of the customer; and
- assess whether entering into the agreement or the increase is responsible.

In order to get a good picture of the financial position of the consumer, the credit provider must have insight into both the consumer's income and certain fixed charges, such as rent or mortgage charges, alimony, etc. A poor financial position (*e.g.* due to an unstable income and high fixed charges) could possibly lead to 'over-indebtedness'. In such a case, the credit provider will not conclude a credit agreement with the consumer

Maximum cost of credit

The cost of credit (interest) is subject to a maximum for consumer credit. The maximum annual cost of credit is the statutory interest rate for non-commercial transactions (which is determined annually) with a surcharge of 12% (Art. 4:35 FSA in conjunction with Cost of Credits (Loans) Decree (*Besluit kredietvergoeding*)).

75 *Offering units in investment funds*

When managing and offering units in investment funds, additional conduct of business rules apply that relate to the manager's business operations and the provision of information (Section 4.3.1.4 FSA). The most important are set out below. Many of these rules are further specified in the MCSD, which in turn refers to AIFMD or its Implementing Regulation. This method of reference is referred to as 'dynamic implementation'.

In view of the great similarity between AIFs and UCITS, we will only discuss the rules for AIFs below.

Requirements to the AIFM

There are a number of organisational requirements for the AIFM, including that it must:

- be a legal entity;
- be headquartered in the Netherlands; and
- have at least two natural persons determining its policy (Art. 4:37c(1-3) FSA).

An investment company does not need to have a separate manager if its equity is at least € 300,000.

Notification procedure and offer requirements

Before the manager may offer units in an AIF, he must provide the AFM with the following information (Art. 4:37c(7) FSA):

- a programme of operations which specifies the AIF it concerns and where the AIF is established;
- the fund rules or the articles of association;
- the name of the AIF's depositary;
- a description of the AIF or, if applicable, the information about the AIF available to participants;
- in the case of a feeder-AIF, information about the domicile of the master-AIF;
- the prospectus; and
- if applicable, arrangements that prevent the marketing of units to retail investors.

A feeder-AIF is an AIF that invests at least 85% of its assets in a master-AIF.

The AFM must notify whether the units may be offered, no later than twenty days after receipt of this information.

Depositary

Appointing a depositary

An AIFM must appoint a depositary for each AIF (Art. 4:62m FSA). This depositary may, however, act as a depositary for several AIFs. The depositary must be established in the same country as the AIF.

For the avoidance of confusion, this depositary is often referred to as the 'AIFMD depositary'. Holding the legal ownership to the assets of an investment fund may also be done by the AIFMD depositary but is usually done by a separate entity established for that purpose (Art. 4:37j FSA; see below).

The function of the AIFMD depositary goes beyond just holding the assets. The tasks of the AIFMD depositary include, *inter alia*:
- cash flow control;
- valuation of units;
- ensure that the sale, issuance, repurchase and redemption of units is carried out correctly; and
- verification of ownership of acquired assets.

Quality and establishment requirements depositary

The depositary must meet quality requirements. Only banks, investment firms or other types of institutions subject to prudential regulation and ongoing supervision can be appointed as a depositary (Art. 4:62n FSA). In case of certain specific types of AIFs, other institutions may be appointed as depositary. This concerns AIFs that are closed-end for at least five years and fall within one of the two following categories (Art. 4:62n FSA in conjunction with Art. 2:3h FSA):
- AIFs which do not invest in assets that must be held in custody (*e.g.* real estate or ships); and
- AIFs that invest in companies with the intention of acquiring control (*e.g.* in private equity).

This depositary is referred to as an 'alternative depositary'. Alternative depositaries are subject to additional requirements:
- they have to be registered with a legally recognised professional register; and
- they must have adequate financial safeguards and professional competence.

Liability of the depositary

In principle, the depositary is liable for any damages to the manager, the AIF and the participants as a result of the loss of financial instruments held in custody and any other damages. This follows explicitly from the AIFMD and has not been implemented in the Netherlands because the legislator felt that this was already provided for by the regulation on breach of contract under Art. 6:74 of the DCC. Art. 4:62p FSA does provide for liability in the event of loss of financial instruments held in custody and outsourcing. In the event of loss of a financial instrument held in custody, the depositary must immediately replace the lost financial instrument with a financial instrument of the same type or reimburse a corresponding amount to the AIF.

If the depositary outsources activities, it remains liable. This also applies if this third party (the sub-depositary) outsources its deposit task to a third party.

Legal ownership of assets

Depositary entity

The legal ownership of the assets of an investment fund must (as it does not have legal personality) be held by a separate entity, whose sole statutory purpose is to hold the assets of one or more investment funds (Art. 4:37j(1) FSA). The reason for this limited purpose is to minimise the insolvency risk of the depositary entity. This depositary entity is different from the 'depositary' (see above). Usually, this is referred to as the 'titleholder' and the depositary referred to in Art. 4:62m FSA as the 'AIFMD depositary'.

The AFM can grant dispensation from this obligation on request (Art. 4:37j(3) and (9) FSA).

Separate depositary entity

If there is a high likelihood that the assets of the investment fund and the equity of the depositary entity will be insufficient to satisfy the allowed claims on the AIF (see below), the legal ownership of the assets of an investment fund must be held by an entity with the sole statutory purpose of holding the legal ownership of the assets exclusively for the benefit of that particular investment fund (whether or not together with the custody and administration of the assets) (Art. 4:37j(2) FSA).

Allowed claims

The assets of the AIF are separate capital and serve exclusively to satisfy claims arising from:

- debts relating to the management, custody and holding of the legal ownership of the assets and which, according to the information provided to participants, may be charged to the capital of the AIF; and
- units (Art. 4:37j(5) FSA).

Creditor ranking

If the assets of an AIF are insufficient to satisfy all the allowed claims, the equity of the AIF shall be used to satisfy these claims in the order as set out above (Art. 4:37j(6) FSA).

Subsequently, the remaining claims may be paid from the assets of the depositary entity itself, again in the order shown above, with due observance of the statutory priority rules (Art. 4:37j(8) FSA).

However, if it is clear that:

- all claims of the AIF can be fulfilled; and
- such claims will not arise in the future,

other claims will be also recoverable from the assets of the AIF (Art. 4:37j(7) FSA).

Valuation of assets

An AIFM must value assets of the AIF and determine the net asset value per unit. This requirement is further laid out into five obligations for the AIFM. The AIFM must:

- establish procedures for the valuation of the assets of the managed AIFs;
- at least once a year, value the assets or have the assets valued by an external valuer;
- at least once a year, determine the net asset value per unit;
- ensure that the articles of association or the fund rules of the AIF state in which manner the participants are informed about the valuation and the net asset value;
- inform the participants of the valuations and the net asset value (Art. 4:37k FSA).

These obligations are further elaborated in Art. 115i MCSD, which is no more than a reference to AIFMD.

Net asset value is calculated by dividing equity by the number of outstanding shares.

Prospectus

An AIFM who wishes to offer units in an AIF in the Netherlands must provide investors with a prospectus in advance (Art. 4:37l FSA).

The prospectus must meet the requirements set out in Art. 115x MCSD. Units in closed-end AIFs (see No 7) qualify as securities and will consequently need to prepare a prospectus in accordance with the Prospectus Regulation instead (see No 79).

Provision of information – professional or retail investors

In addition to the prospectus, an AIFM must also provide other information. A distinction is made in this respect between information for professional investors and information for retail (non-professional) investors. The offers to the latter category are subject to more rules than the offers to the former. Together, these rules are also referred to as the 'top-up regime' (Section 10.3 MCSD). This regime constitutes of, *inter alia*:

- having a so-called 'incident policy' relating to events that pose 'serious threat' to sound business operations;
- professional competence requirements for client-facing employees;
- the calculation of the net asset value of the units;
- equal treatment of participants;
- dispute resolution, KiFID membership;
- a prohibition on cold calling and churning;
- having a website (of which the address is stated in the prospectus, the annual report and the biannual accounts) on which certain information must appear, including:
  - the net asset value (whenever units are offered, purchased or reimbursed); and
  - the terms and conditions (including in which manner it will be published when an exit option exists);
- the preparation of a Key Investor Information Document (**KIID**); and

- providing the financial statements, the annual report, the other information and the biannual accounts to the AFM and publishing them on the website.

Under the top-up regime, investors who acquire units for at least € 100,000 also qualify as 'professional investors' (Art. 4:37p(1) FSA). They are supposed to be 'sufficiently competent and professional and not in need of extra protection'.

Control over undertakings

There are specific rules for AIFMs that acquire control over undertakings (Section 4.3.1.4a FSA). Firstly, it is important that different definitions apply to this section (Art. 4:37q FSA). In case of an unlisted issuer there is 'control' if the AIF can directly or indirectly exercise more than 50% of the voting rights in the general meeting of shareholders.

In the case of a listed issuer, the limit is the threshold for the mandatory bid: 30% (Art. 5:70 FSA; see No 85).

This paragraph does not apply to 'small non-listed companies'. Those are companies with:
- less than 250 employees;
- an annual turnover of less than € 50 million; or
- an annual balance sheet total of less than € 43 million.

Notification obligation

The AIFM must report to the AFM when it acquires 10%, 20%, 30%, 50% and 75%, respectively, of the voting rights in an unlisted company (Art. 4:37s FSA).

These rules are very similar to the reporting rules with regards to listed companies (issuers) in Chapter 5.3 FSA (see No 82).

Information provision

If an AIF acquires control, the manager must inform the shareholders of the non-listed company, the AFM and the non-listed company itself as soon as possible but no later than ten working days thereafter (Art. 4:37t FSA). In that notification, the manager shall include at least the following information:

- the resulting situation with respect to the voting rights;
- the conditions under which control was acquired, including information on the identity of the various shareholders involved, any natural or legal persons who may exercise voting rights on their behalf and, where applicable, the chain of undertakings through which the voting rights are exercised; and
- the date on which the control was acquired.

Asset stripping

Asset stripping is prohibited (Arts. 4:37v FSA and 4:37z FSA). This prohibition means that, for a period of 24 months, the manager may not instruct distributions of profits, capital reductions and redemption of its shares to the undertaking in which the investment firm acquires control. These rules apply to both non-listed and listed companies (issuers).

76 Intermediation

Credit

It is forbidden for a credit intermediary to accept remuneration or compensation, in any form whatsoever, from anyone other than the credit provider (Art. 4:74 FSA). There are a number of exceptions to this prohibition, *e.g.* for mortgage loans (Art. 152 MCSD).

Furthermore, the intermediary must provide pre-contractual information if he is involved in the conclusion of the credit agreement (Art. 4:74a FSA and Art. 4:33 FSA; see No 74).

Insurances

An insurance intermediary must have a professional liability insurance or a similar arrangement (Art. 4:75 FSA). This obligation is further specified in the MCSD (Arts. 159 MCSD and 160 MCSD). This obligation does not apply to banks or insurance companies licensed by DNB and insurance intermediaries with their seat in another Member State (Art. 4:75(4) FSA). In addition, dispensation may be granted by the AFM.

77 Providing investment services

Day-to-day policymakers

The day-to-day policy of an investment firm must be determined by at least two natural persons who work from the Netherlands (Arts. 4:83 FSA and 4:84 FSA).

Asset segregation

An investment firm must take appropriate measures in the context of the custody of financial instruments for clients:

- in order to protect the rights of clients on the funds and financial instruments belonging to them; and

- to prevent the use of those funds or financial instruments by the investment firm for its own account, unless the relevant client has expressly agreed to this (Art. 4:87 FSA).

The purpose of this rule is to separate financial instruments of clients from the assets of the investment firm, so that creditors of the investment firm cannot seek recourse on those assets in the event of insolvency.

This requirement is further specified in Arts. 58, 165 to 165g MCSD, Arts. 47 and 49 Delegated Regulation on Organisational Requirements and in Arts. 7:15-7:20 FRSCFU, determined by the AFM on the basis of Art. 165(2) MCSD.

Art. 58 MCSD and Arts. 47 and 49 Delegated Regulation on Organisational Requirements contain disclosure obligations concerning the measures taken by the investment firm to protect the financial instruments it holds for its clients. These obligations vary according to whether the clients of the investment firm are retail or professional investors.

Arts. 165-165g MCSD contain substantive rules on the custody of financial instruments. An investment firm:

- must keep all records and accounts that are necessary to immediately enable a distinction between financial instruments and funds which are held for a client from financial instruments which are held for other clients and the investment firm's own financial instruments (Art. 165(1)(b) MCSD);
- must regularly confirm whether the information and accounts correspond to those of any third parties who may hold these financial instruments and funds (Art. 165(1)(c) MCSD);

- must ensure that financial instruments held with a third party can be distinguished from the financial instruments belonging to the investment firm and financial instruments belonging to third parties (Art. 165(1)(d) MCSD);
- must exercise due care, meticulousness and diligence when appointing a third party, taking into account the third party's expertise and market reputation (Art. 165a(1) MCSD);
- if the custody of financial instruments is subject to specific regulation in the jurisdiction where it wants to keep the financial instruments, may not transfer the financial instruments to a third party which is not subject to supervision of compliance therewith (Art. 165a(2) MCSD); and
- may not hold financial instruments with a third party in a non-EEA member state where the custody of financial instruments is not regulated, unless (a) the nature of the financial instruments or the investment services to be provided requires this or (b), if it concerns financial instruments held for a professional investor, the client has requested this in writing (Art. 165a(3) MCSD).

The investment firm may only enter into repos and securities lending transactions in respect of financial instruments held by the investment firm on behalf of clients if:

- the client has expressly agreed in advance to the conditions; and
- this is exclusively done in accordance with those conditions (Art. 165c MCSD).

Repo is an abbreviation of repurchase agreement and is a transaction whereby securities are temporarily sold for trading or liquidity purposes and repurchased on a predetermined date at a predetermined price.

Once a year, an investment firm must submit a report by an external auditor to the AFM on its compliance with the asset segregation rules (Art. 165d MCSD).

Conflicts of interest

Investment firms may engage in different activities relating to financial instruments, which may give rise to conflicts of interest. Therefore, an investment firm must pursue an adequate policy for the prevention and management of conflicts of interest between itself and its clients and between its clients (Art. 4:88 FSA). Arts. 33 and 34 of the Delegated Regulation on Organisational Requirements set out the requirements for this policy in more detail, which provide that the policy must be aimed at recognising the following specific situations:

- the investment firm or employee may make a financial gain or avoid a financial loss at the expense of the client;
- the investment firm or employee has a conflicting interest in the result of a transaction on behalf of the client or in the execution of a transaction on behalf of the client;
- the investment firm or employee has a financial, or any other motive to put the interest of another client or group above the interest of the client;
- the investment firm or employee is in the same business as the client; and
- the investment firm or employee receives a commission that differs from the usual commission or fee from a person other than the client (Art. 33 Delegated Regulation on Organisational Requirements).

If a conflict of interest is unavoidable, an investment firm must treat the client fairly and inform the client before proceeding to do business (Art. 167 MCSD and Art. 34(4) Delegated Regulation on Organisational Requirements).

Informing clients should be considered a last resort. In principle, the policy should aim to prevent conflicts of interest.

Duty of care

An investment firm has a general obligation to act honestly, fairly and professionally in accordance with the interests of its clients and to refrain from conduct that is detrimental to the integrity of the market (Art. 4:90 FSA). This general standard for investment firms is laid down and further specified in the FSA and the MCSD. Because of the fact that the duty of care for investment firms is explicitly laid down in the FSA, the AFM may supervise this. This is separate from the civil duty of care and procedures in that context. Civil judges will take the general duty of care under Art. 4:90 FSA into consideration and, more generally, the conduct of business rules in Part 4.

Best execution

When executing orders in financial instruments on behalf of clients, an investment firm must take sufficient steps to obtain the best possible result for clients (Art. 4:90a FSA). This is referred to as the best execution obligation.

The following considerations are important in determining the best possible result:

- the price of the financial instruments;
- the execution costs;
- the speed, the likelihood of execution and settlement; and

- the size, nature or any other consideration relevant to the execution of the order.

The investment firm must then determine the relative weight of these factors:
- the characteristics of the client, including its 'classification';
- the characteristics of the order;
- the characteristics of the financial instruments that are the subject to that order; and
- the characteristics of the execution venues where that order can be executed (Art. 64(1) Delegated Regulation on Organisational Requirements).

What best execution is, can, therefore, differ per order/client.

The best execution obligation does not apply if a client gives a specific instruction for an order.

To comply with the best execution obligation, the investment firm must have a policy in place and monitor compliance with this policy (Art. 4:90b FSA). This policy shall include information on execution venues and considerations affecting the choice of execution venues for each class of financial instruments. It shall, in any case, specify the execution venue which enables the investment firm to obtain the best possible result for the execution of client orders on a consistent basis.

In addition, the investment firm must specify in this order execution policy how it determines the relative weight of the various factors (Art. 66(1a) Delegated Regulation on Organisational Requirements).

If an investment firm transmits orders to another entity (a broker), it must also take all reasonable steps to obtain the best possible result for the client. This situation will also have to be included in the policy (Art. 65 Delegated Regulation on Organisational Requirements).

The investment firm should provide its clients with clear information on its order execution policy. This information should explain in a clear, sufficiently precise and comprehensible way for clients how the investment firm will execute orders on behalf of its clients (Art. 4:90b(3) FSA).

The policy must be evaluated annually by the investment firm (Art. 66(1) Delegated Regulation on Organisational Requirements).

Finally, an investment firm must process client orders chronologically. Therefore, earlier submitted client orders must be prioritised over later client orders or the trading portfolio of the investment firm itself (Art. 4:90d(1) FSA).

Transaction reporting

Investment firms are required to report their transactions in financial instruments admitted to trading on a regulated market to the AFM as soon as possible and at the latest before the end of the next business day (Art. 26(1) MiFIR). It is important to note that a transaction can be both a 'purchase' and 'sale' of a financial instrument. The information which needs to be provided can be found in the directly applicable MiFID Implementing Regulation (No 1287/2006). The AFM has a tool for this reporting requirement, by means of which investment firms can report.

Special provisions

Arts. 4:91a-4:91q FSA contain specific provisions concerning, among other things, the management of OTFs, MTFs, SME growth markets, systematic internalisation, algorithmic trading, direct electronic access, clearing institutions and insurance-based investment products.

78 *Relationships between financial firms*

Providers versus intermediaries and authorised (sub)agents

Before a provider wants to work with an intermediary for the first time, it must ensure that the intermediary is appropriately licensed and acts in accordance with the FSA (Arts. 4:94 FSA and 4:97 FSA). As such, financial firms are used to ensure compliance with the FSA in the distribution chain.

In any event, the provider must do this check once a year or when the provider receives signals that raise concern. If the broker indeed acts in breach of the FSA, the provider must cease its relationship with that intermediary.

A provider may no longer enter into agreements with an intermediary or authorised agent to whom a prohibition as referred to in Art. 1:58(2) FSA or Art. 4:4(1) FSA has been imposed. Agreements already entered into may, in certain cases, be settled with the assistance of the involved intermediary or authorised agent (Art. 1:104(3) FSA or Art. 4:4(2) FSA).

The same applies to a provider who uses an authorised agent (Art. 4:95 FSA) and to an intermediary or authorised agent who intermediates or acts on behalf of a provider (Art. 4:96 FSA). If a provider notes that an intermediary or authorised agent acts in breach of Arts. 4:9 , 4:10 , 4:15 , 4:74b or 4:75 FSA, it must immediately report this to the AFM. If a provider notes that another provision of the FSA is systematically breached, it must also report this to the AFM immediately. Financial firms must allow each other to comply with these obligations.

Parties can report via the AFM's digital portal. In addition, the AFM has published a Guideline on the Notification Obligation of Providers.

A provider who reports a breach is not liable for damages suffered by a third party as a result of the report, unless it is demonstrated that he should not reasonably have made such a report, taking into account all circumstances (Art. 4:98 FSA).

Relationships between investment firms and versus tied agents and AIFs

The same system applies to the relationship between investment firms (Art. 4:100 FSA) and the relationship between investment firms and tied agents (Art. 4:100b(2) and (3) FSA and Arts. 4:100c-4:100e FSA).

In addition, the investment firm is obliged to notify the use of a tied agent to the AFM prior to the provision of services (Art. 4:100b(1) FSA).

An investment firm offering units in AIFs must confirm prior to the offer whether the units may be offered in accordance with the FSA (Art. 4:100f FSA).

Insurers versus intermediaries and authorised (sub)agents

In the relationship between an intermediary and an insurer, an insurance which has been established through intermediation or which has been transferred to the portfolio of an intermediary, belongs to the portfolio of the intermediary as long as the insurance is not transferred from its portfolio (Art. 4:102 FSA). An insurer may not transfer (part of) its portfolio to another intermediary without the permission of the intermediary (Art. 4:103 FSA).

In principle, in the case of non-life insurances, the intermediary will collect the premiums, but the insurer may in some cases stipulate that the intermediary is no longer entitled to collection, unless contractually agreed otherwise (Art. 4:104 FSA).

An investment firm offering units in AIFs must confirm prior to the offer whether the units may be offered in accordance with the FSA (Art. 4:100f FSA).

VII Part on Market conduct supervision of financial firms (Part 5)

79 *Rules for the offering of securities*

Since 21 July 2019, the prospectus requirement has been removed from Chapter 5.1 FSA and the Prospectus Regulation (Regulation (EU) No 2017/1129) applies directly within the EU. Since the rules concerning the offering and listing (admission to trading on a regulated market) of securities are essential within the supervisory framework for financial markets, the relevant rules are nevertheless discussed here.

The obligation to publish a prospectus

It is forbidden to:

- offer securities to the public within the EU; or
- to admit securities to trading on a regulated market situated or operating within the EU,

unless an approved prospectus has been published in accordance with the Regulation (Art. 3(1) and (3) Prospectus Regulation).

The article shows that both activities are in themselves prohibited without an approved prospectus, unless a statutory exception or exemption applies.

The prohibition applies to transferable securities, except for money market instruments, as defined in MiFID:

- shares in companies and other securities similar to shares in companies, as well as depository receipts for shares;
- bonds and other debt instruments as well as depository receipt for such securities;
- any other securities giving the right to acquire or sell any such transferable securities or giving rise to a cash settlement determined by reference to transferable securities, currencies, interest rates or yields, commodities or other indices or measures (Art. 4(1)(44) MiFID);
- 'offer of securities to the public': *a communication to persons in any form and by any means, presenting sufficient information on the terms of the offer and the securities to be offered, so as to enable an investor to decide to purchase or subscribe for those securities. This definition also applies to the placing of securities through financial intermediaries* (Art. 2(d) Prospectus Regulation),
- 'admitted to trading on a regulated market': *in short, the listing of securities on a regulated market* (see No 81). Therefore, the prohibition does not apply to a listing of securities on an MTF (*e.g.* Tradeweb EU B.V.).

General exceptions

The Prospectus Regulation does not apply to the following types of securities:

- units issued by collective investment undertakings other than the closed-end type (see No 10);
- non-equity securities issued by a member state's regional or local authorities, by public international bodies of which one or more member states are members, or by central banks of the member states;
- shares in the capital of central banks of member states;

- securities unconditionally and irrevocably guaranteed by a member state or its local or regional authorities;
- securities issued by associations with a legal status or non-profit institutions in order to achieve commercial objectives; or
- non-fungible shares of capital whose main purpose is to provide the holder a right to occupy an apartment, or other form of immovable property or part thereof where the shares cannot be sold without relinquishing that right (Art. 1(2) Prospectus Regulation).

Please note that there is a prospectus requirement for open-end AIFs and UCITS in Part 4 of the FSA (see No 75).

Specific exceptions

The obligation to publish a prospectus shall not apply to, *inter alia*, the following types of offers of securities to the public:

- an offer of securities addressed solely to qualified investors;
- an offer of securities addressed to fewer than 150 natural persons or legal entities per member state, other than qualified investors;
- an offer of securities whose denomination per unit amounts to at least € 100,000;
- an offer of securities addressed to investors who acquire securities for a total consideration of at least of at least € 100,000 per investor; or
- shares issued in substitution for shares of the same class already issued, if the issuing of such new shares does not involve any increase in the issued capital (Art. 1(4) Prospectus Regulation).

More specific exceptions to the obligation to publish a prospectus apply, for example, in the case of:

- securities offered in connection with a take-over by means of an exchange offer;
- securities offered, allotted or to be allotted with a merger or division;
- dividends paid out to existing shareholders in the form of depositary receipts for shares;
- securities issued to current or former directors, current or former members of the supervisory board or current or former employees; or
- certain types of non-equity securities issued by a credit institution, where the total aggregate consideration in the EU for the securities offered is less than € 75,000,000 per credit institution (Art. 1(4) Prospectus Regulation),

each to the extent that the applicable conditions are met.

Exceptions to the obligation to publish a prospectus for admission to trading on a regulated market are set out in Art. 1(5) Prospectus Regulation. Examples are securities which are fungible with securities already admitted to trading on the same regulated market, provided that these securities represent less than 20% of the number of securities already admitted to trading on the same regulated market over a period of twelve months, certain securities resulting from the conversion or exchange of other securities, and securities offered in connection with a takeover by way of a public offer of exchange, provided that certain information requirements are met (Art. 1(5) Prospectus Regulation).

Exemptions

In addition, there is an exemption for securities that are part of an offer of which the total consideration within the EEA, calculated per category and over a period of twelve months, is less than € 5,000,000 (Art. 3(2) Prospectus Regulation in conjunction with Art. 53 FSA Exemption Regulation). If there are multiple offers within a group of affiliated companies, the considerations of the respective offers are added up for the purpose of this exemption. If an offer of securities to the public relies on this legal exemption, the offer must be notified to the AFM prior to the offer, while simultaneously providing the information referred to in Art. 53(3) FSA Exemption Regulation using the documents listed in appendix a of the FSA Exemption Regulation.

The offeror is required to include an exemption legend in its marketing materials if it makes use of this exemption and the offer is not only addressed to qualified investors (Art. 53(4) FSA Exemption Regulation). A standard legend should be included, which is also known as the 'wild west sign':

Figure 3 The 'wild west sign'

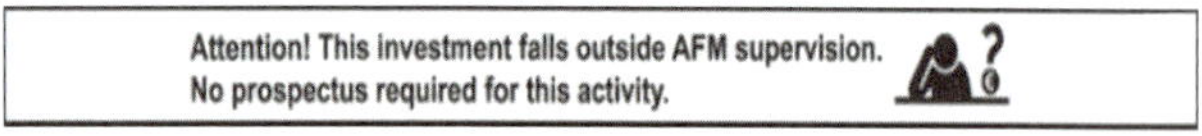

A similar sign exists for exemption from the licence obligation for AIFMs (see No 32).

Approval authority

A prospectus must be approved by the competent authority of the home member state. Which authority is competent to approve a prospectus depends on:

- the place where the issuer has its seat;

- the place where the securities are offered to the public or admitted to a regulated market; and
- the type of securities (equity or non-equity) and the nominal value per security (greater or smaller than € 1,000).

The home member state is:
- where it concerns an issue of non-equity shares with a nominal value per security of at least € 1,000:
  - the member state in which the issuer has its seat; or
  - the member state chosen by the issuer, the offeror or the one requesting admission to trading on the regulated market where the securities are or will be admitted to trading on a regulated market or where the securities are offered to the public,
- where the above does not apply:
  - the member state in which the issuer has its seat, if the issuer is established in the EU; or
  - the member state where the securities are offered to the public or admitted to trading on a regulated market for the first time, if the issuer is not established in the EU (Art. 2(m) Prospectus Regulation).

In the Netherlands, the competent authority is the AFM.

Approval procedure

The procedure for approval of the prospectus can be found in Art. 20 Prospectus Regulation. For example, the competent authority must decide on an application for approval within ten business days (Art. 20(2) Prospectus Regulation). For an initial public offering (IPO), whereby securities of an undertaking are listed for the first time on a regulated market, a period of twenty days applies (Art. 20(2)

Prospectus Regulation). If the application is incomplete, the competent authority may ask for supplementary information. In such case, the time limit will only apply from the date on which the supplementary information is provided (Art. 20(4) Prospectus Regulation).

European passport

If a prospectus has been approved by the competent authority, the issuer may ask the competent authority to certify that the prospectus has been drawn up in accordance with the Prospectus Regulation (Art. 25 Prospectus Regulation). This certificate of approval can be used as a European passport, so a prospectus does not have to be approved in other member states. This is similar to the European passport for licences (see No 25).

Content, form and language of the prospectus

Content

The prospectus shall contain such information as is essential to enable investors to make an informed assessment of the assets and liabilities, profits and losses, financial position and prospects of the issuer and of any guarantor, the rights attached to these securities and the reasons for the issue and its impact on the issuer (Art. 6(1) Prospectus Regulation).

What information this concerns, can be found in Arts. 13-19 of the Prospectus Regulation and its annexes.

Certain information may be included in the prospectus by cross-reference (e.g. to the issuer's audited financial statements), provided that the requirements of Art. 19 Prospectus Regulation are met.

Form

The prospectus itself consists of:

- a single document with a summary that complies with Art. 8 Prospectus Regulation; or
- three different documents (Art. 10 Prospectus Regulation):
  - a registration document containing information on the issuer;
  - a securities note containing information about the securities offered to the public or for which a request for admission to trading on a regulated market is made; and
  - a summary in accordance with Art. 7 Prospectus Regulation.

The advantage of the three documents is that in case of a new issue requiring an approved prospectus, an issuer does not always need to update its registration document, but a new summary and a new securities note may suffice.

Language

In principle a prospectus must be written in a language accepted by the competent authority of the home member state. For the AFM this is Dutch or English. In the case of cross-border offers of securities, the prospectus shall be drawn up in a language accepted by the competent authorities of those member states or in a language customary in the sphere of international finance (Art. 27(1) and (2) Prospectus Regulation). An exception to this rule applies to the admission to trading on a regulated market (situated in the Netherlands or in another member state) of non-equity securities with a denomination per unit of at least € 100,000 (Art. 27(5) Prospectus Regulation).

Advertisements

An issuer, an offeror or someone requesting the admission of securities to trading on a regulated market shall ensure that an advertisement:

- indicates that a prospectus is generally available and where it can be obtained; and
- is recognisable as such and contains information which is not inaccurate or misleading and in accordance with the information contained in the prospectus (Art. 22(2) and (3) Prospectus Regulation).

General availability

Once approved, the prospectus must be made available to the public in accordance with the requirements of Art. 21 Prospectus Regulation (Art. 21(1) Prospectus Regulation). The prospectus must be made generally available within a reasonable period of time prior and before the offer of the securities to the public or the admission of the securities to trading on the regulated market.

Period of validity of the prospectus

A prospectus is valid for twelve months after its approval for offers of securities to the public or admission to trading on a regulated market (Art. 12 Prospectus Regulation).

80 *Rules for information provision by issuers*

The information obligation

Issuers whose securities are admitted to a regulated market have certain (ongoing) information obligations, which can be found in

Arts. 5:25a-5:25w FSA. These can be divided into periodic and incidental information obligations.

Scope of application/home member state

Many (but not all) obligations only apply to issuers whose home member state is the Netherlands. These can be either Dutch or foreign entities.

For the determination of the home member state, Art. 5:25a FSA refers to Art. 2(1)(i) of the Transparency Directive. Schematically this looks like this:

Table 5 Determination of the home member state

Issuer of (i) debt securities with a denomination per unit of less than € 1,000 (or equivalent value in another currency) or (ii) shares.	**EEA Institution**: the member state in which it has its seat. **Institution from outside the EEA**: The member state elected by the institution from the member states in which its securities are admitted to trading on a regulated market.
Issuers of other securities than those listed above	**EEA Institution**: can chose between: – the member state in which it has its seat; and – the member states in which its securities are admitted to trading on a regulated market.
	Institution from outside the EEA: the member state elected by the institution from the states where its securities are admitted to trading on a regulated market.

The issuer must disclose what its home member state is to:

- the competent authority of the member state in which it has its seat;
- the competent authority of the home member state; and

- the competent authorities of all member states where the issuer's securities are admitted to trading on a regulated market (Art. 5:25a(3) FSA).

If the issuer has not disclosed its home member state within three months, it shall automatically be the member state where its securities are admitted to trading on a regulated market.

Periodic obligations

Annual financial reporting

An issuer must publish its annual report within four months after the end of its financial year (Art. 5:25c FSA). This is a shorter term than in Book 2 of the DCC.

The annual report of an issuer must include:

- the audited financial statements;
- the management report; and
- statements by those persons designated by the issuer as being responsible for the truth and fairness of the issuer's financial statements and management report.

Five days after adoption of the financial statements, the adopted financial statements and the management report (including the information appended thereto pursuant to Art. 2:392 BW) must be submitted to the AFM by the issuer (Art. 5:25(1) FSA).

Biannual financial reporting

An issuer must draw up its biannual report and make it generally available as soon as possible, but no later than three months after the end of the first six months of its financial year (Art. 5:25d FSA).

The biannual report of an issuer shall include:

- the biannual financial statements;
- the management report; and
- statements by those persons designated by the issuer as being responsible for the truth and fairness of the issuer's financial statements and management report.

If the biannual financial statements have been audited, the auditor's report will be published together with the biannual report, and if the biannual financial statements have not been audited, this will be reported in the management report (Art. 5:25d(2) and (3) FSA).

Incidental obligations

An issuer must promptly provide information on changes to shareholders' or bondholders' rights, including (for the latter group) changes to the conditions (Art. 5:25h FSA).

Statutory exceptions

The information obligations apply exclusively to issuers:

- whose securities are admitted to a regulated market; and
- of which the Netherlands is the home member state (Art. 5:25b(1) FSA).

They do not apply to open-end AIFs and UCITS (Art. 5:25b(3) FSA).

The incidental obligations do not apply to:

- states, regional or local government bodies, the ECB, etc;
- issuers who exclusively issue bonds or other non-equity securities with a denomination per unit of at least € 100,000; and

- issuers who exclusively issue debt securities already admitted to trading on a regulated market in the EU before 31 December 2010 and whose denomination per unit amounts to at least € 50,000 (Art. 5:25g FSA).

Information about meetings

An issuer must make the following information and documents available to shareholders:

- information about the general meeting when convening the meeting;
- information about the total number of shares and voting rights attached to them at the start of the general meeting;
- an authorisation (proxy) form (Art. 5:25k(2) FSA);
- authorisation to a bank to satisfy claims of shareholders;
- information about the payment of dividends; and
- information about issuing new shares (Art. 5:25k(4) FSA).

The issuer must make this information, as well as any draft resolutions, available on the website no later than 42 days before the day of the general meeting (Art. 5:25ka(1) FSA). No later than fifteen days after the general meeting, the issuing institution must publish the voting results on its website (Art. 5:25ka (3) FSA).

Similar rules apply to the disclosure of information to bondholders.

81 *Rules for access to Dutch markets for market operators and for managing a regulated market*

Prohibition

It is prohibited to operate or manage a regulated market in the Netherlands without a licence from the Minister of Finance (Art. 5:26 FSA).

A regulated market is defined as *'a multilateral system which brings together or facilitates the bringing together of multiple third-party buying and selling interests in financial instruments – within that system and in accordance with its non-discretionary rules – in a way that results in a contract, in respect of the financial instruments admitted to trading under its rules and systems, and which operates regularly and in accordance with the applicable rules regarding licensing and continuous supervision'.*

Examples in the Netherlands are *Euronext Amsterdam*, *ICE Endex* or *Nxchange*.

The same prohibition applies to an auction platform for emission allowances as referred to in chapter VII of Regulation (EU) No 1031/2010 (Art. 5:25x FSA). Only two of these exist in Europe: *the European Energy Exchange* in Germany and the *ICE Futures Europe* in the United Kingdom.

Statutory exemption and dispensation possibility

The prohibition does not apply to the operation or management of a regulated market:

- with its seat in another member state;
- authorised by the competent authority of another member state; and

- insofar as the relevant market operator makes appropriate provisions in the Netherlands in order to enable members or participants to access and trade on this market from the Netherlands.

In addition, the Minister of Finance can grant dispensation from the licence obligation (Art. 5:26 FSA).

Rules of the regulated market

A market operator must ensure that the regulated market:

- has rules and procedures in place to identify and manage potential negative consequences of conflicts of interest between the regulated market, the owners and the market operator;
- is adequately equipped to manage the risks to which it is exposed;
- has rules and procedures for the sound management of the technical functioning of its system;
- has transparent, non-discretionary rules and procedures to ensure fair and orderly trading;
- has effective rules and procedures to ensure effective and timely handling of transactions executed through its systems;
- has sufficient financial resources to promote the orderly functioning of the market, taking into consideration the nature and size of transactions executed on the market and the nature and size of the risks to which it is exposed (Art. 5:30 FSA); and
- has effective rules and procedures in place to regularly monitor and to ensure that members or participants of the regulated market comply with these rules on an ongoing basis (Art. 5:32 FSA).

Rules for the admission of financial instruments

A market operator should set rules:

- on the admission of financial instruments to trading on the regulated market;
- to facilitate the access of the members or participants of the regulated market to public information (see below);
- to regularly verify:
  - whether the financial instruments meet the eligibility requirements; and
  - that issuers comply with their initial, ongoing and incidental information obligations (see Nos 80 and 82). This relates, for example, to checking the availability of a prospectus or annual financial statements (Art. 5:32a FSA).

Rules for access to the regulated market

A market operator must set transparent and non-discriminatory rules, based on objective criteria, for the access to trading on or becoming a member of the regulated market, and to ensure the effective enforcement of these rules (Art. 5:32b FSA).

Suspension of or exclusion from trading

A market operator can agree in the agreement with the issuers (the 'listing contract') in which cases it can suspend or exclude a financial instrument from trading. The market operator exercising this right also does so with respect to derivative instruments. However, it may not do so if such a measure could significantly undermine the interests of investors or the orderly functioning of the regulated market (Art. 5:32g FSA). If it wishes to exercise this right, it must inform the AFM accordingly.

A market operator can also be instructed by the AFM to suspend or interrupt trading of a certain financial instrument for a certain period of time (Art. 1:77d FSA). This is a far-reaching power that the AFM can only use under exceptional circumstances.

Disclosure obligation (pre-trade)

A market operator shall make public:

- current bid and offer prices which are advertised through their systems; and
- the depth of trading interest at those prices (Arts. 3 and 4 MiFIR).

This information must be available at all times during trading hours. This concerns pre-trade transparency.

Disclosure obligation (post-trade)

A market operator also has a duty to disclose:

- the price;
- the volume; and
- the time of the transactions that are executed via the regulated market in the shares admitted to trading (Art. 5:32k(4) FSA).

This information must be shared in 'real' time as much as possible, unless the AFM has granted a postponement at request. This concerns post-trade transparency.

These disclosure obligations only apply to shares admitted to trading on the regulated market and its purpose is to enable investors and other market participants to verify the conditions under which the transaction was carried out *a posteriori*.

82 *Rules for disclosure of votes, capital, control and capital interest in issuers*

There are three types of disclosures relating to issuers:

- notifications by issuers on capital and votes (Art. 5:34 FSA);
- notifications on shares and votes by shareholders and other persons entitled to vote (Art. 5:38 FSA); and
- notifications on shares and votes by executive board members and supervisory board members (Art. 5:48 FSA).

The applicable rules are set out in more detail in the DMHD.

Deviating definitions and scope

The following definitions (deviating from Art. 1:1 FSA) included in Art. 5:33 FSA are essential in determining the scope of the disclosure obligations:

- '**Issuers**' are:
  - Dutch public limited liability companies (*naamloze vennootschappen*) whose shares are admitted to trading on a regulated market within the EEA;
  - legal entities from another member state whose shares are only admitted to trading on a regulated market in the Netherlands; or
  - legal entities from a non-EU member state whose shares are admitted to trading on a regulated market in the Netherlands.

An issuer is not a closed-end investment company or a UCITS company (Art. 5:33(2) FSA).

- '**Capital**' is the issued capital of the issuer including shares that have been redeemed, but not yet withdrawn.
- '**Shares**' are not exclusively shares within the meaning of Art. 2:79 DCC, but also depositary receipts for shares, and other instruments giving a right to acquire shares, such as convertible bonds and options.
- '**Votes**' are the voting rights attached to shares. It is important to note in this context that votes held by other parties can also be attributed in some situations (*e.g.* in the case of a voting agreement).

Notification by issuers

Issuing institutions must notify changes in their issued capital to the AFM (Art. 5:34 FSA). Changes in the issued capital may occur, for example, when new shares are issued, as a result of which the capital is increased, or by withdrawing redeemed shares, as a result of which the capital is reduced. Changes of more than 1% must be reported immediately by the issuer. Other changes may be reported on a periodical basis.

In addition, issuers must notify the AFM if:

- the number of votes attached to outstanding shares changes; or
- depositary receipts for shares are issued or withdrawn with its cooperation (Art. 5:35 FSA).

The AFM keeps a register in which the outstanding capital per issuer can be found (Art. 5:49 FSA).

Notifications by shareholders and other persons entitled to vote

Anyone who acquires or disposes of shares or voting rights must immediately notify the AFM if this results in reaching, exceeding or falling below the threshold values of the total number of shares or the total number of votes (Art. 5:38 FSA).

The notification obligation also applies with respect to capital or voting rights when 'passively' reaching, exceeding or falling below the thresholds as a result of a change by in the capital or voting rights by the issuer (see above) (Art. 5:39 FSA).

The threshold values are 3%, 5%, 10%, 15%, 20%, 25%, 30%, 40%, 50%, 60%, 75% and 95%, with a so-called 'substantial holding' as of 3%.

In addition to these reports for so-called 'long positions', 'short positions' must also be disclosed (Arts. 5:38(3) and 5:39(2) FSA). Short positions are positions used to speculate on a decrease of the value of shares in an issuer. These positions are taken by buying a 'put option' (a financial instrument that gives the right to sell shares at a predetermined value at a certain time). The regime for short positions is the so-called 'gross short regime'.

The absence of a notification regime for gross short positions is an important omission, as became apparent from the disclosure of 4 May 2012 by investment bank Morgan Stanley regarding an economic interest in KPN. This notification did disclose the gross long position of Morgan Stanley in KPN but did not include information on any gross short position of Morgan Stanley. Market parties were unaware about the extent to which Morgan Stanley was economically exposed and whether the short position was perhaps as large as the long position (Parliamentary History II 2011/12, 32014, No 34).

In addition, there is the 'net short regime'. A net short position is the position that remains after the long position has been deducted from the gross short position. The net short regime is laid down in the Short Selling Regulation (Regulation (EU) No 236/2012).

Finally, there is a disclosure obligation for AIFMs and UCITS management companies. The basis for this can be found in Chapter 4. These are notification obligations in respect of listed issuers and non-listed issuers (see No 75).

Attribution of shares or votes

For the calculation of the number of shares or votes that must be disclosed, also shares or votes that are attributed to someone based on factual circumstances should be taken into account (Art. 5:45 FSA).

For example:
Because a voting agreement has been entered into with a third party, because subsidiaries also hold shares or votes or because it concerns a manager of an investment fund (an entity without legal personality).

Exceptions

A number of exceptions have been included for notifications by shareholders and other persons entitled to vote under special circumstances (Arts. 5:46 and 5:47 FSA).

For example:
For custodians of shares, to the extent that the shares and the votes attached thereto are held in the exercise of their business and the voting rights cannot be exercised at their discretion. In addition, for non-member state issuers, in some cases the first threshold is 5% instead of 3%.

Disclosures by directors and supervisory directors

Management board members and supervisory board members of listed Dutch public limited liability companies must disclose all votes and shares they hold in the issuer of which they are a management board member or supervisory board member to the AFM (Art. 5:48 FSA). No thresholds apply in this context. Management board members and supervisory board members must also report shares and votes in 'affiliated issuers'. This includes:

- other issuers with which the issuer is linked in a group or in which it has a holding, provided that the turnover of that other issuer is at least 10% of the turnover of the issuer itself; and
- other issuers having an interest of at least 25% in the issuer.

Consequences of non-compliance

If no disclosure is made, the issuer, other holders of a 'substantial holding' (3% or more of the shares or votes) and holders of shares with special rights under the articles of association may initiate special civil proceedings before the court (Art. 5:52 FSA). Measures that can be imposed by the court are, for example:

- an injunction not to increase his interest for a maximum period of five years;
- a suspension of voting rights for a maximum period of three years; or
- nullification of resolutions of the general meeting of shareholders if those resolutions could not have been made

without the exercise of the voting rights by the one that was required to disclose its position.

83 Rules to prevent market abuse

Since the entry into force of the Market Abuse Regulation (Regulation (EU) No 596/2014, **MAR**) on 3 July 2016, the FSA no longer contains rules to prevent market abuse. Because this Boom Basics would not be complete without a description of these rules, the most important rules from MAR are described below.

Prohibition to use inside information

It is prohibited to use inside information (Art. 14 MAR). Use of inside information concerns the execution or arrangement of transactions in financial instruments (in short: dealing) or cancelling or adjusting such a transaction.

Case law of the Court of Justice on the Market Abuse Directive provides that a person that has inside information is 'deemed to use it' in a transaction. This is a rebuttable presumption but does not require proof as such in the first instance (ECJ 23 December 2009, case C-45/08, Spector Photo Group).

MAR contains a comprehensive description of the concept of inside information, which specifies that it concerns information that meets the following four conditions:

- the information has not been made public;
- the information is precise;
- the information relates to one or more issuers or financial instruments; and

- the information, if it were made public, would be likely to have a significant influence on the price of the concerning financial instruments.

Primary and secondary insiders

The prohibition on the use of inside information shall apply to all shareholders, but distinguishes two categories therein:

- **Primary insiders**: persons who have a special relationship with the issuer, *e.g.* management board members and supervisory board members or persons who have a qualifying holding in the issuer. It is irrelevant whether the persons designated as primary insiders know, or should reasonably suspect, that they have inside information. They are presumed to possess it.
- **Secondary insiders**: all persons other than primary insiders. For secondary insiders it must be proven that they know or should reasonably suspect that the knowledge that they possess is inside information.

Tipping off ban

Also, a ban on disclosing that inside information with others or recommending any other person to deal applies (Art. 10 MAR).

Prohibition on market manipulation

Furthermore, it is prohibited to manipulate or attempt to manipulate the market (Art. 15 MAR). Market manipulation occurs for example:

- in case of transactions and orders which may give false or misleading signals as to the supply of, demand for or price of financial instruments;
- in case of transactions and orders with the intention to secure the price at an artificial level. This so-called 'price stabilisation'

occurs for example, when (large) buy orders are placed to prevent a decrease in the price of financial instruments. This can be done with the use of so-called 'high frequency trading' techniques;
- by disseminating false or misleading information that may give an incorrect or misleading signal as to the supply of, demand for or price of financial instruments; and
- with other forms of fraud or deception.

See Art. 12 MAR, but also Annex I to MAR for several examples.

Other disclosure and notification obligations

Issuers must draw up a list of persons who may regularly or occasionally possess inside information (an 'insider list', Art. 18 MAR). The issuer should inform the persons on that list of the prohibition to use inside information, the prohibition to tip off, the prohibition of market manipulation and the consequences of any breach thereof.

In addition, managers and compliance officers of an issuer must report all their transactions in the financial instruments issued by the issuer to the AFM (Art. 19 MAR).

And finally, there is a duty to report. MAR requires any person professionally executing transactions in financial instruments (banks and investment firms) to report suspicious orders and transactions (Art. 16 MAR). This means that if that person has a reasonable suspicion that an order or transaction in a financial instrument may involve (attempted) insider dealing or market manipulation, he or she must immediately notify the AFM.

84 *Securities-related market conduct of business supervision*

Certain financial firms that trade in financial instruments must comply with specific rules relating to the sound management of their business, the so-called securities-related market conduct of business supervision (Art. 5:68 FSA).

A person within the organisation must be charged with the monitoring of compliance with these rules (Art. 22(1) MAD). This will usually be the compliance officer.

Scope

The securities-related market conduct of business supervision applies to financial firms with an office (*i.e.* seat or branch) in the Netherlands. It concerns, *inter alia*:

- banks;
- AIFMs and UCITS management companies;
- AIFs and UCITS;
- investment firms;
- pension funds; and
- insurers.

In addition, it covers trading in financial instruments on both a regulated market and on an MTF or OTF (see No 10).

Inside information and market abuse

A financial firm must take adequate measures to:

- prevent inside information from becoming available outside the circle of persons who, by virtue of the exercise of their profession or function, are required to possess the information (Art. 21s(a) MAD); and

- ensure that persons connected with the undertaking exercise the utmost care in dealing with information which they know or should reasonably know to be inside information (Art. 21(b) MAD).

In addition, appropriate procedures must be in place to enable employees to report MAR breaches internally (Art. 22(2) MAD).

Cluster munitions

A financial firm must take adequate measures to prevent:

- executing or giving orders for execution of transactions with the purpose of acquiring or offering a financial instrument issued by an undertaking that holds, produces, sells or distributes cluster munitions, or crucial parts thereof;
- granting loans to such an undertaking; and
- acquiring non-transferable holdings in the capital of such an undertaking (Art. 21a(1) MAD).

Code of conduct for private transactions and prevention of conflicts of interest

Certain financial firms are required to have a code of conduct for private transactions on the financial markets by persons linked to the undertaking who are directly involved in the undertaking's transactions in financial instruments or who otherwise regularly (may) possess inside information on a professional basis (Art. 24 MAD). This code of conduct must contain additional rules for 'insiders' (Art. 25(1) MAD). These are management board members, persons whose activities consist of executing transactions and other persons who (may) regularly possess inside information (Art. 25(2) MAD).

The code of conduct must also stipulate that the persons identified must avoid any mixing of business and private interests in relation to transactions (Art. 26 MAD).

Statutory exemptions

The securities-related market conduct of business supervision does not apply to:

- certain AIFs or UCITS (Art. 56(1) FSA Exemption Regulation);
- group finance companies as referred to in Art. 3:2 FSA (Art. 56(2) FSA Exemption Regulation); and
- a specific category of non-life insurers (Art. 1:10(a) FSA in conjunction with Art. 15 PSFD).

85 *Public bids for securities*

Mandatory public bid

Anyone who, whether or not acting in concert with others, can exercise predominant control over a listed public limited liability company with its seat in the Netherlands, is obliged to make a public bid (Art. 5:70 FSA). Predominant control means at least 30% of the voting rights in a general meeting of shareholders (Art. 1:1 FSA).

A public bid is '*the making of an offer to the investors by means of a public announcement as referred to in Art. 6:217(1)* DCC *or inviting the investors to make such an offer to the bidder*'. The offer must be made in public because the potential buyer will not know who all the shareholders in the listed undertaking are.

This rule protects the other shareholders from the predominant control that the shareholder can exercise.

Publication

In addition, the holder of predominant control must, after the acquisition of predominant control:

- make a public announcement on this subject without delay (Art. 5:72a FSA); and
- announce the public bid within thirty days (Art. 5:70 FSA). The announcement is made by publication of a press release.

Statutory exemptions

The mandatory public bid does not apply to, *inter alia*, those who:

- acquire predominant control in an open-end investment company (whether or not a UCITS), *because of the exit option;*
- acquire predominant control through declaring a public bid unconditionally, who as a result thereof can exercise more than 50% of the voting rights, *because of the fact that there was an exit option;*
- are an anti-takeover foundation which, after the announcement of the public bid, will hold the shares for a maximum period of two years protecting the target undertaking;
- are independent administration offices that have issued depositary receipts for shares with cooperation of the undertaking;
- acquire predominant control in connection with a group transfer of the predominant control, *because a restructuring and reorganisation should not be unnecessarily obstructed;*
- maintain predominant control at the time of an IPO, *because of the fact that shareholders who acquire the shares at that time are aware*

of the interest and influence of the major shareholder of the listed undertaking; and
- are a custodian of shares, to the extent that it cannot exercise the voting rights attached to the shares at its own discretion (Art. 5:71 FSA).

Grace rule

A second exception applies if the holding is reduced to less than 30% within thirty days. In that case, the holder of the predominant control may make use of the so-called grace rule (Art. 5:72 FSA). This means that no mandatory bid needs to be made if the following two conditions are met:
- the reduction of the position may not be realised by a transfer to someone covered by one of the abovementioned exceptions; and
- the holder of predominant control is not allowed to exercise voting rights during the grace period.

Exemption Regulation

Exempt under Art. 2 TBED are, *inter alia*, those:
- who, alone or acting in concert with others, directly or indirectly acquire predominant control:
  - with the consent of 90% of the general meeting (with the exception of the acquirer and persons acting in concert);
  - as a result of 'underwriting' (see No 10); or
  - by agreeing to 'irrevocable undertakings'; and
- acquiring control at the same time with someone else, and the number of voting rights attached to the control is equal for both (Art. 5:71(i)(h) FSA).

Consequences of non-compliance

If no public bid is made, the target undertaking and the other holders of shares in the target undertaking may initiate special civil proceedings before the Enterprise Chamber of the Amsterdam Court of Appeal to take measures (Art. 5:73 FSA). Measures that can be imposed by the Enterprise Chamber include:

- an obligation to make a bid;
- a suspension of voting rights for a specified period of time;
- a prohibition to participate in general meetings; or
- annulment of a resolution of the general meeting.

Fair price

A public bid must be made at a 'fair price'. In principle, the fair price is the highest price paid by the bidder in the year preceding the announcement of the mandatory bid (Art. 5:80a FSA). Contrary to this, the Enterprise Chamber may determine the fair price on request (Art. 5:80b FSA).

The judgment as to whether someone is required to make a bid and the authority to determine the fair price, therefore, lies with the Enterprise Chamber and not with the AFM. As soon as a mandatory bid is announced, it is subject to the supervision of public bids by the AFM and the bidding process described below applies to it (with minor exceptions).

Offer memorandum obligation

Regardless of whether the public bid is mandatory (as discussed above) or voluntary, bidding rules apply to ensure an orderly and transparent bidding process. As such, it is prohibited to make a public bid without an offer memorandum that has been made generally available and has been approved by the AFM (Art. 5:74(1) FSA).

Exemption

An exemption applies in case it concerns:

- a public bid for securities to which no voting rights are attached directly or potentially (with the exception of non-convertible depositary receipts); or
- the repurchase of previously issued securities issued by the bidder (Art. 56a FSA Exemption Regulation).

Approval of the offer memorandum

The bidder must submit a request for approval of the offer memorandum within twelve weeks of the publication of the public bid.

The AFM is authorised to approve the offer memorandum if the securities of the target undertaking are listed on a Dutch regulated market and the target undertaking has its seat in:

- the Netherlands;
- another member state and the securities;
  - are not also listed in that member state;
  - are also listed in yet another member state but the
  - securities are first listed in the Netherlands;
  - are also listed in that member state and the target undertaking is an *open-end AIF*;
  - are listed simultaneously and for the first time in the Netherlands and in a member state other than that in which the target undertaking has its seat and the target undertaking elected the AFM for approval; and
- a non-member state (Art. 5:74(2) FSA).

The AFM assesses the offer memorandum for compliance with the requirements set out in the PTBD (Art. 5:76(1) FSA). The appendices to the PTBD provide non-exhaustive lists of the information that must be included in the offer memorandum, *e.g.* the bid price, the conditions for declaring the offer unconditional and the period in which shareholders can register to accept the offer.

Timelines

The AFM must announce its decision within ten working days after receiving the application (Art. 5:77(1) FSA). If the AFM approves the offer memorandum, the applicant must make the offer memorandum generally available within six days (*i.e.* make the public bid) or announce that it will not make a public bid (Art. 5:78 FSA).

The period during which shareholders can register to accept the offer commences between the first business day following the public bid and nine business days after the approval of the offer memorandum by the AFM (Art. 14 PTBD).

The bidder must announce whether the bid will be declared unconditional, no later than on the third business day after the end of the registration period. If so, this will result in the conclusion of a purchase agreement between the bidder and all shareholders who have registered (Art. 16 PTBD).

86 *Code of conduct for institutional investors*

Institutional investors (see No 9) with their seat in the Netherlands that invest in listed undertakings are required to report on their compliance with the principles and best practice provisions of the Dutch Corporate Governance Code (Art. 5:86 FSA) that are addressed to them.

With this requirement, provisions for institutional investors included in the Corporate Governance Code are legally anchored in the FSA. The aim is to increase transparency, particularly vis-à-vis the underlying beneficiaries, about the institutional investors' voting policies.

This means that they must publish annually on their website or in their annual report about:

- the voting policy (best practice IV.4.1);
- the implementation of the voting policy (best practice IV.4.2); and
- the votes cast at the general meetings (best practice IV.4.3).

If they fail to comply with the principles and best practice provisions of the Dutch Corporate Governance Code addressed to them, they must state their reasons, in accordance with the 'comply or explain' principle. This is also subject to the annual disclosure requirement.

Exemption

There is an exemption for (often from a licence obligation exempted) AIFMs and UCITS management companies (Art. 57 FSA Exemption Regulation).

VIII Part on Special measures relating to the stability of the financial system (Part 6)

87 *Immediate measures and expropriation*

Immediate measures

Under special circumstances, the Minister of Finance, after consulting DNB and in agreement with the Prime Minister, has the authority to take immediate measures in respect of a financial firm (Art. 6:1 FSA). DNB is consulted because it has a better view on the financial position of financial firms due to its task as prudential regulator.

Special circumstances

Special circumstances exist where the situation of the financial firm poses a serious and imminent threat to the stability of the financial system. As such, it must be an acute threat, as a result of which there is no time to await, for example, the outcome of consultations with the management board of the financial firm.

The danger must be specific and not just a risk. For example:

- the threat of no longer being able to meet the minimum solvency requirements;
- an (acute) liquidity deficit;
- problems in group relations;
- the refusal of other parties to allow the undertaking to continue participating in the flow of credit; or
- a strong decline in the public's confidence in the financial firm.

The size of the undertaking is not decisive. The decisive factor is whether the financial firm's situation has consequences for the stability of the financial system. This is particularly relevant for systemic banks.

'Immediate measures'

Immediate measures are (orderly) measures which must be justified on the grounds of strengthening the position of the financial firm and thereby preventing or reducing a serious threat to the stability of the financial system. For example:

- the appointment of a supervisory board member with a veto on matters relating to the (improvement of the) financial situation of the undertaking. It is not intended that the Dutch State should take over the management of the undertaking, which should remain with the undertaking itself;
- suspending or dismissing current management board members and appointing new management board members;
- the suspension of resolutions already taken by one of the undertaking's bodies; or
- the temporary suspension of a right of approval of the of holders of (priority) shares with respect to a resolution that is crucial for the improvement of the undertaking's situation. Should the relevant resolution already have been taken, it could be suspended.

Derogation from the law or articles of association

Immediate measures may be taken in derogation from the law or the articles of association. This concerns for instance:

- the corporate law provisions of Book 2 of the DCC;
- any blocking or other protective measures in the articles of association of the concerned undertaking;

- the Securities Giro Act (*Wet giraal effectenverkeer*) (in the context of expropriation); or
- the FSA itself (*e.g.* with regard to the bidding rules, as referred to in Art. 5:70 FSA *et seq.*).

It is not possible to derogate from Part 6. Otherwise, the safeguards around the Minister's powers could be avoided.

Expropriation

Instead of immediate measures, the Minister may also expropriate:

- assets (assets and liabilities) of the undertaking; or
- securities issued by or with the cooperation of the undertaking, (*e.g.* shares in the capital of the undertaking, convertible bonds or perpetuals) (Art. 6:2 FSA).

This is considered to be an ultimate remedy.

The far-reaching measures were applied for the first time in the Netherlands when SNS was nationalised in 2013. The bank (SNS Bank) and the insurer (SNS Reaal) were both in dire straits. SNS Bank had been appointed by DNB as systemically relevant and when it became apparent in January 2013 that SNS Bank would not be able to overcome the financial problems on its own, the Minister had roughly two options:

- *let SNS Bank go bankrupt; or*
- *expropriation on the basis of Part 6.*

The Minister opted for the second option: expropriation of all shares, subordinated bonds and private debts of SNS Bank and SNS Reaal (Resolution 1 February 2013, FM 2013/213).

The starting point is that assets or securities are transferred to the Dutch State by way of expropriation, but they may also be transferred to a civil law legal entity.

'This was chosen because it may be desirable to separate the assets or securities acquired through expropriation from the assets of the State at the time of expropriation and thus not to give rise to any liability on the part of the State for debts that are part of the assets involved in the transaction' (Parliamentary History II 2011/12, 33 059, No 3).

Expropriated assets or securities are transferred unencumbered (Art. 6:2(6) FSA). Rights of pledge, mortgage rights or rights of usufruct on those assets or securities and, to the extent known, the attachments made on them do not lapse, but transfer to the right to compensation (Art. 6:8(3) FSA). This construction is derived from the statutory rules from Art. 2:92a(8) DCC and Art. 2:359c(9) DCC that apply to share buy-outs.

A combination of expropriation and immediate measures is possible.

Parent undertaking

The measures may also extend to the parent undertaking of the concerning undertaking, provided that that parent undertaking has its seat in the Netherlands (Art. 6:4 FSA).

Notification AFM

The Minister must notify the AFM of any intention or actual decision to take any of the abovementioned measures. In the event of expropriation of securities listed on a Dutch regulated market, OTF or MTF, the AFM must suspend trading in these securities, or related derivatives such as options after the notification (Art. 6:3(2) FSA) by giving the relevant market operator or systematic internaliser an instruction to do so (see No 81).

Restriction of counterparties' rights after immediate measures or expropriation

If the abovementioned measures are taken, the rights of the counterparties of the financial firm will be restricted (Art. 6:5a FSA in conjunction with Art. 1:76b FSA, see No 59).

In case of expropriation, an exception applies for set-off arrangements (*e.g.* in derivative agreements) (Art. 6:2(7) FSA).

88 *Legal protection and compensation*

Legal protection

The FSA provides legal protection when one of the measures described above is taken. Considering the intrusive nature of the measures, it is considered important that a court can issue a judgment in relation to those measures swiftly.

After all, the question of whether the Minister has rightly decided to intervene must not remain unanswered for too long.

Thus:

- a direct appeal is possible and there is no need to first lodge an objection with the Administrative Jurisdiction Division of the Council of State in order for it to act as the highest general administrative court and for a final judgment to be passed immediately; and
- there is a fast judicial procedure in which;

- the appeal must be lodged within 10 days; and
- a decision will be made within two weeks (Arts. 6:6 and 6:7 FSA).

Compensation

When expropriation takes place, the holders of assets or securities in the undertaking concerned lose part of their property. That is why compensation is provided (Art. 6:8 FSA). Parties who had a right of pledge or mortgage on the expropriated assets or securities see their collateral disappear from the hands of their debtors in the event of expropriation. For the benefit of these guarantors, a right of pledge is created over the compensation amount (Art. 6:8(3) FSA). This does, however, almost certainly result in a decrease of collateral for the secured parties.

Mortgage rights cannot be created over the right to compensation, as no mortgage right can be created in respect of such rights. It is therefore stipulated that a mortgage right is converted into a right of pledge (cf. conversion pursuant to Art. 3:42 DCC). The right of pledge will be created over the right to compensation.

- The damage must be a 'direct and necessary' *consequence* of the expropriation. For example, the value lost by a share *prior to its* expropriation as a result of a price drop, will not be eligible for compensation.
- Not the nominal, but only the 'actual value' of the expropriated property is compensated (Art. 6:8(2) FSA). The prospects that the undertaking would have had if no expropriation had taken place must be taken as the starting point. The actual value is the price that, given that prospect, would have been established in a normal sale between two parties 'acting reasonably' (Art. 6:9(1)

FSA). In the case of listed shares (or other securities), it is obvious that it would be appropriate to *also* consider the listed prices of these shares.

- The Minister must make a compensation offer (Art. 6:10(2) FSA) no later than seven days after the expropriation.
- Subsequently, the Enterprise Chamber of the Court of Appeal of Amsterdam must determine the compensation (Art. 6:10(1) FSA).

This ensures that compensation is subject to judicial review in any case, even where an expropriated party is not in a position to submit the compensation for judicial review or for any other reason waives that possibility. If the expropriated parties consider the Minister's offer to be too low, they may, in their defence, request the Enterprise Chamber to determine a higher compensation. The Enterprise Chamber may do so if it deems it plausible that the compensation offered does not constitute full compensation for the damages incurred.

The procedure with the Enterprise Chamber is a normal civil petition proceeding. Therefore, it is possible to appeal to the Supreme Court (*cassatie*).

In the SNS case, the Minister had made an offer of compensation of € 0 per asset or security. In the first instance, the Enterprise Chamber ruled, inter alia, that the offer was too low. In final appeal, the Supreme Court ruled that the valuation takes place on the reference date, i.e. the date of expropriation. In addition, according to the Supreme Court, the actual value must be determined by the price that the parties acting reasonably would have agreed, in view of SNS's objectively established future prospects. That price does not only depend on the market value. The Supreme Court then referred the case back to the Enterprise Chamber, which appointed experts to investigate what would be a reasonable price. The experts should assume a situation in which SNS would not have been expropriated (Supreme Court 20 March 2015, JOR 2015/140 (Minister of Finance/VEB c.s.)).

No later than four weeks after submission of the application for determination of the compensation, the Dutch State will pay the compensation as an advance payment (Art. 6:12(1) FSA). The advantage hereof is that parties do not have to wait for the proceedings with Enterprise Chamber. It is possible that they will be paid even more afterwards, *i.e.* if the Enterprise Chamber ultimately determines the compensation at a higher amount.

Index

Please refer to section numbers.